Praise for

Grow the Tree You Got

"*The most important job in the world to me is the one of Parent. Tom Sturges shares his view on raising kids in a way that made me want to change my Parental Destiny—an amazing and life-changing read!*"

—Kris Jenner, television personality and businesswoman

"*This is a subject of interest to every parent of teenagers, and Tom Sturges tells it like it is, from personal experience.*"

—Hugh Hefner, founder of *Playboy* magazine

"*In order to give our children the best chance at a great life, they need constant guidance, encouragement, love, and support. Tom Sturges's book is a wonderful road map to evolved parenting that everyone will find invaluable.*"

—Clive Davis, Chief Creative Officer, Sony Music Entertainment

"*Tom Sturges is the quintessential modern dad—engaged, committed, sensitive. His observations and recommendations are life-affirming and compassionate. A welcome approach to dealing with adolescence in today's world.*"

—Elaine Wynn, National Chairman, Communities in Schools

GROW *the* TREE YOU GOT

& 99 OTHER IDEAS FOR RAISING
AMAZING ADOLESCENTS AND TEENAGERS

TOM STURGES

JEREMY P. TARCHER / PENGUIN

a member of Penguin Group (USA) Inc.

New York

JEREMY P. TARCHER/PENGUIN
Published by the Penguin Group
Penguin Group (USA) Inc., 375 Hudson Street, New York, New York 10014, USA •
Penguin Group (Canada), 90 Eglinton Avenue East, Suite 700, Toronto, Ontario M4P 2Y3,
Canada (a division of Pearson Penguin Canada Inc.) • Penguin Books Ltd,
80 Strand, London WC2R 0RL, England • Penguin Ireland, 25 St Stephen's Green,
Dublin 2, Ireland (a division of Penguin Books Ltd) • Penguin Group (Australia),
250 Camberwell Road, Camberwell, Victoria 3124, Australia (a division of Pearson
Australia Group Pty Ltd) • Penguin Books India Pvt Ltd, 11 Community Centre,
Panchsheel Park, New Delhi–110 017, India • Penguin Group (NZ),
67 Apollo Drive, Rosedale, North Shore 0632, New Zealand (a division
of Pearson New Zealand Ltd) • Penguin Books (South Africa) (Pty) Ltd,
24 Sturdee Avenue, Rosebank, Johannesburg 2196, South Africa

Penguin Books Ltd, Registered Offices: 80 Strand, London WC2R 0RL, England

Most Tarcher/Penguin books are available at special quantity discounts for bulk
purchase for sales promotions, premiums, fund-raising, and educational needs. Special books
or book excerpts also can be created to fit specific needs. For details, write Penguin Group
(USA) Inc. Special Markets, 375 Hudson Street, New York, NY 10014.

Library of Congress Cataloging-in-Publication Data

Sturges, Tom.
Grow the tree you got : & 99 other ideas for raising amazing
adolescents and teenagers / Tom Sturges.
p.   cm.
ISBN 978-1-58542-860-1
1. Child rearing.   2. Parent and teenager.   3. Parent and adult child.   I. Title.
HQ769.S933   2011   2011002957
649'.125—dc22

Printed in the United States of America
1   3   5   7   9   10   8   6   4   2

BOOK DESIGN BY NICOLE LAROCHE

While the author has made every effort to provide accurate telephone numbers
and Internet addresses at the time of publication, neither the publisher nor the author
assumes any responsibility for errors, or for changes that occur after publication.
Further, the publisher does not have any control over and does not assume any
responsibility for author or third-party websites or their content.

*Penguin is committed to publishing works of quality and integrity.
In that spirit, we are proud to offer this book to our readers;
however, the story, the experiences, and the words
are the author's alone.*

This book is dedicated to Thomas, Sam, and Kian,
my three sons, my three teachers.

contents

INTRODUCTION

I remember the day it hit me that life with Thomas had changed forever. I woke up that morning to the sight of him walking around the house with a pimple on his cheek the size of an M&M. His room smelled slightly of Axe body spray, and every time I needed to talk to him he was behind a locked door. It seemed as if he'd gone to bed a child the night before and woken up an adolescent. "Where did all the time go?" I asked myself, while making a mental note that my collection of semi-provocative magazines (mostly old *Sports Illustrated* swimsuit issues) was no longer in precise chronological order. It crossed my mind that these were minor details and probably nothing to worry about, but in reality they were the overture. The opera was coming next.

Within a few months, the nature and depth of our communication began to change, and the one-word sentence found a place in his repertoire of snappy answers. It was but a harbinger of many short sentences to come.

"How was school today?" I asked my seventh-grader.

"Fine."

"Did you talk to your teacher about that grade you got on your science paper?"

"Yes."

"Anything more you want to tell me?"

"No."

"Mommy says that you might want to go to the fair tomorrow . . . ?"

"Hmmmm . . ." he said to me betwixt mumbling commands to a legion of friends also playing World of Warcraft on the Internet.

"Has anyone spoken to all the other parents?"

"Yeah."

"What will you do with yourselves all day . . . ?"

"Dunno."

"That's almost two words, isn't it?"

"Nope."

"Okay, nice talking to you."

"Okay."

"Love you, son."

"M'too . . ."

A little while later it occurred to me that a lot of time had passed since Thomas had asked me to teach him how to ride a bike. This realization came just about the same time he started asking me to teach him how to drive a car. "Dad, I'm almost thirteen!" he said, not realizing this was probably the last thing that would convince me.

My friends with daughters compared notes with me. Apparently things change just as quickly for girls. One day they're reading *Knitting Digest* or *Highlights*, the next day it's *Vogue* and *Teen People*, and it happens in the blink of a false eyelash. One dad I know sent Twiggy to summer camp, and guess who came back? Pamela Anderson. "Where did my daughter go?" he wondered as he noticed that the girl who looked vaguely like his child appeared to be wearing blush, eyeliner, and possibly some sparkly stuff on her neck and shoulders.

Adolescent and teenage years are an end and a beginning. They are the end of innocence and the beginning of knowing. The end of "Why?" and the beginning of "Why not?" The end of "What if . . . ?" and the beginning of "What now?" The end of "What the heck?" and the beginning of "What the . . . ?" Adolescence arrives and out the window go many of the established rituals between parents and their offspring. It is a whole new ball game, baby. All concerned must now contend with a newly minted pre-teenage smart aleck. He somehow knows everything about everything and never meets a question he cannot answer. As is customary with adolescents, he is often wrong, but always certain. This burgeoning false wisdom signals the dawn of a burning new age. Adolescents urgently need to know where all of the boundaries are, and they need to find out right away, just as soon as possible. Adolescence is all about the present. It is life in the moment. The last thing adolescents want to hear about is the future. Bor-ing. We the parents have no idea what the metamorphosis will bring to our children's lives, our own lives, and, of course, the lives of our snoopy prying neighbors. All that we can do is prepare for everything and anything that might occur, and then hope that we have prepared enough. If your child is within shouting distance of eleven, it's time to get started.

There are many wonderful books on parenting, of course, but none I read were exactly right. I wanted to provide my sons with something different. I wanted to raise them to be truthful and generous and wonderful people, but not change who they were meant to be, and not alter in any way their unique gifts, whatever those might turn out to be.

The first hurdle was time. How could I possibly find the time it takes to be a great dad while also earning a living, caring for an aging parent, trying to keep a marriage to-gether, and finding a few minutes for myself every now and again? I realized early on that there is no such thing as qual-ity time, there is only quantity time. So every extra mo-ment, every free moment, every available moment went first to the boys, and once they were exhausted and the cup was full, I had a moment for me. With no time to spare, I also realized that I had to make the most of the time I had. That is how this book came to life. It is first and foremost my guide for *me*, my crib notes to keep me always on track to be the father I still dream I can be.

If an idea or technique worked well, I would write it down and try it again and again. If I stumbled across something another parent did that was particularly ingenious or exemplary, I kept notes so that I could try the same thing when I needed another option. Rule #5: Call Me, No Questions Asked builds an unshakable trust between parent and teenager and has proven to be perfect for me and Thomas. Mercifully, he needed it only twice. Rocks in the Roots is a strategy for getting through tough times with an adolescent. It has never failed me, either as a parent or as a mentor. The entirety of the section "Big Dreams" is about how dreams of an amazing future can be such a vitally important part of the arc of life for adolescents and teenagers.

As they grow, they change, and there are always new challenges. The one I faced that surprised me most was the realization that many of the connections between me and my boys could be easily disrupted or even broken down completely, by divorce, for instance. It was almost too late when I saw that there needed to be many more opportunities for us to be together, and I had thought I had plenty.

The ideas that grew from trying to maintain those vital and beautiful connections became The Seven Bridges Rule and Someday May Already Be Here.

Coincidentally, another dad told me how everything changed between him and his daughter, not because of a divorce, but because he was unable to properly anticipate what she needed and what she was going through. One night he said good night to her and they shared a couple of secrets of the day, just like they had for many years. But the next night, she thought that he was prying and spying, and she demanded her privacy and would not share anything at all with him again, for *years*. Although he was hurt, he did the right thing: *nothing*.

A father cannot take it personally, nor can he reject his daughter simply because she has rejected him. She has no more control over what is causing her to react that way than he does. The father has to accept this new version of his daughter in all respects, her emotional, intellectual, passionate, and newly dreaming self. She is growing up and he must come to terms with that. The father's goal should be to keep her trusting him and trusting in him as long as possible. The longer she stays close to her father, the longer it will take her to replace him with the next great love of her life. The template for many of her friendships and love affairs is her relationship with her father. The father needs to make every effort to win her over, and win her back, again and again, repeatedly, with kindness, with forgiveness, with love. Watching great parents deal with these central issues of their lives with daughters became the basis of the rule Ordinary People—Extraordinary Parents and the rule Fathers and Daughters.

There is not *one* type of adolescence. Each child's adolescence is different, an experience unique beyond measure, unmappable until it is very clearly in the rearview mirror. Some are harmless jaunts and others take your breath away. My own adolescence was not ideal by any means, but because of that I was ready for anything that could happen with my own boys. The old saying "Anything can happen, at any time" is not so old that it is out-of-date. Anything *can* happen. It might not even have been invented yet, or be something you even consider a possibility, but events can spiral out of control so quickly, regardless of whether or not you thought it could happen to you. Several families I interviewed for this book needed to send their children to a tough-love boot camp. The discussion of Had We the Chance to Do It Over Again concerns what they would have done differently. For all of them, the onset of their problems was a quick surprise, and the aftermath was like bad opera—slow and never-ending. They were able to recover some semblance of a life only *after* their children got sober, got clean, and decided to rejoin the human adventure. They were kind enough to share their views and the wisdom gained from their experiences and to criticize themselves, possibly helping other families avoid the events that nearly dragged their families under.

There is much at stake when it comes to the challenge of raising adolescents and teenagers. One wrong move can send a life hurtling off in an entirely unintended direction, and one small piece of wisdom can bring it back just as fast. You never know when your child is listening, and you can never know what of your, ahem, genius, if any, will get through to them. Life is not a science, it is an art. Raising adolescents and teenagers is like modern art. It will take the very best of you just to understand what is being asked of you. More than likely everything will turn out okay, give or take a few quarts of adrenaline over the years.

Have faith in your teenager. Provide as much freedom as you dare. Build big dreams. Expect great things. Be patient with the stumbles and forgiving of the mistakes. Only rarely will bad happen on purpose. Recognize when things have gone well and reward those efforts with practical gifts, like forgiveness when things do *not* go so well. Be a great listener. Be understanding. Be generous with your praise and stingy with your criticism. Be kind and be loving. Share the best of you.

But more important than anything else, help your children first discover who they are supposed to become, and then help them become those people. Whoever or whatever that turns out to look like, one of your first promises as the parent should be to encourage and enable them to become the very best version of themselves they can possibly be. Actor, lawyer, or dancer. Athlete, musician, or doctor. Redwood, oak, or acacia, maple, spruce, or pine.

Grow the tree you got.

PART ONE

GETTING STARTED

The adolescent and teenage years are a great challenge for people on both sides of the equation, not only for the child/young adult but for all of the rest of us too. Paul Boerger, in his book *Your Teenager Is Insane*, has written that the hormones, growth spurts, and other life forces brought to bear on adolescent children actually make them insane. I could not disagree more.

My son Thomas described this period in his life this way: "I felt *bigger* than everyone else . . . hypersensitive, hormone-riddled." He soared to "new highs and devastating lows."

Patience, kindness, listening, anticipating, understanding, risking love, putting the adolescent first and absolutely first, putting your frustrations last, absolutely last—these are just a few of the basic requirements that should be met when the time comes to begin one of the most complicated and beautiful journeys available. Here are some others.

THE PAUL McCARTNEY RULE

❧

Paul McCartney. One of the greatest writers and singers and performers of this or almost any other generation. How many treasures like him do we have in the world? His songs will live forever, his voice is a signpost to millions of us, his concerts are among the greatest ever given, his charity and his devotion to his family are legendary, and his life is iconic. Videos of his various performances have been seen almost 2 billion times on YouTube and MySpace. From his first days with the Beatles, to his nearly two decades in Wings, to these recent years as simply Sir Paul McCartney, he has spent his entire adulthood in the limelight. Ups, downs, awards, recognition, wealth, disappointments, great achievements, arrests, rumors, his supposed death, the loss of his beautiful wife, a divorce, all of it played out in the public view.

Anyone who has had so much of his life exposed to the world could have a lot of things to be embarrassed about.

GROW THE TREE YOU GOT

For example, Paul McCartney was the person who suggested to Michael Jackson that he get into the music publishing business, and then lost the copyrights to his own songs when Jackson heeded his advice and bought the Beatles' song copyrights. He never said a word about it. Paul McCartney was the one who told the world he did not need a prenuptial agreement before marrying Heather Mills. Within a very brief window of time, the new Mrs. McCartney got pregnant, had a child, filed for divorce, and stung him for $50 million or so before she packed up her things and sauntered right out of his life. If it bothered him, you would never know it. He refused to say anything that would make anyone think that he was capable of feeling any regrets. He is simply that kind of man.

Years ago, his first wife, Linda (née Eastman), was playing with Paul in his band Wings. They toured the world together several times, raised their children, and lived as a family despite the extraordinary challenges that life on the road presented. Onstage, Linda was not the musician or singer that Paul was. Though this was a known fact throughout the musical universe, Paul refused to make a change. He loved her being onstage with him and did not really care if she was that great a singer or not. One unkind sound engineer isolated her vocal mike during a concert, recorded it, and gave it to several radio stations in an attempt to embarrass everyone. On the particular night the recording was made, her contributions to "Hey Jude" were possibly not so great. She was a little off-key perhaps, or might have been singing a different song. Whatever. Confronted with this during an interview, Paul waved off the question as if it did not even deserve the time it would take to answer. Next.

As far as I can tell, he doesn't look back, he never looks back. He has never let his past get in the way of his present or his future. He simply will not let it. Sir Paul McCartney never says anything about anything. He steadfastly refuses to be embarrassed about himself, his actions, his choices, his music—frankly, by anything at all. I love this about him and I have let this wisdom from his life slip into my own. "No embarrassments" is a philosophy I keep with me, particularly as it relates to my adolescent and teenage children. I might be upset that someone did not try his hardest on a big test. I might be miffed that my birthday was overlooked, again. I might be disappointed that somebody's GPA is lower this year than it has ever been before. But I follow the Paul McCartney Rule, and never am I embarrassed by anything my boys do. They are part of me, and that's all there is to it.

Perhaps your children do not get the straight A's you had hoped for. Perhaps they are not the sports prodigies you asked the fortune-teller about before you got married. Perhaps they are just as socially awkward as you were when you were their age. Be proud of them no matter what, in each and any and every circumstance. Let them always know how thrilled you are that they turned out to be just who they are. They are your creation, your gift to the world.

If you find yourself in a circumstance with your children and you are not sure how to act, or react, or even respond to what they have done, ask yourself: What would Paul McCartney do? Nothing! Never again be embarrassed by anything your teenager has done, should have done, should not have done, is doing, should not be doing, is wearing, should not be wearing, and so forth. Leave it alone. Look the other way. Let it go. Let It Be.

LEARNING TO LET GO,
A LITTLE

~⁕~

I was sitting with my then twelve-year-old Thomas at dinner, just the two of us. As the conversation unfolded, the hair on the back of my neck was starting to stand up. I could not help it, nor could I believe the words that were coming out of his mouth. He wanted more what? More space in his life? More time on his own? What? It was like the band was breaking up, and re-forming, without *me*. Without me? I suddenly knew what Pete Best must have been feeling all these years.

Thomas was in the middle of telling me that he needed more room to operate, more time to be himself, more space, and, basically, less me. Me, his soccer and basketball and baseball coach, chauffeur, message and package delivery service, masseur, minor-injury miracle worker, and party organizer . . . ? He needed more time away from me? I was the person who almost never turned down a request, who was happy to role-play concierge to his hotel guest. All of these years, whatever he needed, I tried to get for him, as long as he asked me nicely. But he did not want any of that suddenly; he needed more space. If I had been wearing a hearing aid, I would have pulled it out and checked the batteries.

We were in a restaurant and he was looking at me just a little too sympathetically. Getting to the conclusion of his statement, very sweetly he said these words: "Dad, I think it's okay for you to have your own friends again."

It took me a minute to get my emotional balance back, to find my bearings and to realize what was happening and what had just happened. The caterpillar was clearly nearing its chrysalis stage. My little boy had begun to recognize that he needed a change in his life, that he was now ready to move to the next stage, and maybe he was not so little a boy anymore.

I knew exactly what he was asking for, even if he did not know exactly. Yes, of course it broke my heart, a little. Yes, it made me sad. Yes, I felt rejected and unimportant. But I also knew that this was part of his coming-of-age and that he had found a way to tell me what he needed. I told him that I wanted to think about it. In trying to come to terms with his request, I searched my own memories and came face-to-face with an experience from my own adolescence and teenage years that guided me in how to act in this situation.

Synanon in the 1970s was a drug rehabilitation center that also offered a preventative program for non-addicts. Because I was growing up in Hollywood in the middle of the hippie era, my mother was terrified that I would become a drug addict. I was thirteen and had taken nothing stronger than aspirin, but my mother bought the "preventative" part of the story completely. It turned out to be a well-played scam and she lost her house in the arrangement. Two and a half years later, when I was fifteen years old, I ran away and was reunited with her. In the time since we had last lived together, I had changed completely. Gone forever was the innocent child she had sent away for safekeeping. Outgrown forever were all of the clothes that she had so carefully packed for me. Lost forever was her fair-haired dreamer, the little boy who used to watch the skylight for his lost Daddy-boy to meet him somehow, somewhere, someday. The prodigal son who showed up on her doorstep the day I returned had grown up on his own, without her. I now possibly had hair on my chest and even a ghost of a mustache. But more fundamentally, I had survived living in a very close association with a community of ex–drug addicts, ex-parolees, ex-alcoholics, ex-hookers, ex–con men, and many of their just-as-streetwise children, plus the occasional innocent like me whose parents had fallen for the same ruse.

I think of this time in my life as Prehab.

Planned or not, I had been fending for myself, providing for myself, figuring out angles, trying to determine a vision of my future, creating my own big dreams and avoiding the bad choices, and I had been doing this for years. The very last thing that I needed was a doting mother to make a thousand suggestions and get in the way of all that I had learned. As far as I was concerned, I did not need her that way anymore. Those days were gone. It took less than a week of being back home with her for me to realize that it was not working. I knew that something had to change.

I sat with my mother one night after she came home from work. I remember knowing that I was going to ask for something very difficult, and reminded myself to be sure to be very respectful. I told her that I was not the boy she remembered, nor was I the man I was to become—I was balanced kind of in the middle. I didn't know *how* I knew, but I knew that I did not need the same kind of mothering that I had needed when we were together before. I had outgrown that kind of relationship. However difficult it must have been for her to hear the words, she did something brilliant and amazing as we were sitting there: She listened to me. She heard me. She let it in.

I asked her to let our relationship change into something else, to let it grow up and mature, not as an accident, but as a conscious decision that we made, together. I told her that I needed a less-doting mother and more of a best pal. I needed fewer helpful suggestions about my hygiene and more support of my attempts to find a job. I needed less snooping and more roommate, less suspicion and more trusting. I needed more space to be me, and to *become* me.

A couple of days later, courageous and gracious, vulnerable but still proud, she agreed to my request. She said okay. Everything changed forever. I wanted more territory and she was the only person in the world who could give it to me. By listening to me and letting us change, she allowed me the freedom to live with her, be with her, and enjoy the pleasure of her company forever, with my guard down, my defenses disarmed. I knew that she would never knowingly embarrass me in front of my friends, ask where I had been every minute, or inhibit me from considering any dream. She became my most faithful and trusted ally and my dearest friend. There was a peace that began that evening that will survive for the rest of our lives.

Although the words were a little different, Thomas's request was remarkably similar to the one that I had made to my mother many years before. I knew exactly how he felt. Exactly. It was as though time had just folded in on itself. Like

I was picking up a favorite book and it fell open to the page where I had left off reading it years before.

After a few days, I agreed to his request to give him more of the space that he needed. He started to enjoy a few more freedoms, though not so much as to leave him room to get in any serious trouble, and he was never so far away that he was not within easy grasp, both literally and figuratively. I gave him a little more wiggle room. I was not going to punish him for making the request, nor was there even a breath of resentment that I was no longer the number-one pal in his life, no matter how badly I wished that I still was.

Once our new arrangement began, I discovered an unintended consequence. By showing Thomas the respect he requested and allowing him the opportunity to make sense of his adolescence, I realized that I could start to make a little better sense of my own. By making his adolescence simpler to live through, I could make mine a little less difficult to look back on. By forgiving him for pushing me away, I could forgive myself for pushing my mother away. If a little less of me in his life was required for all of those good things to happen, then so be it. It was a sacrifice that, once I understood it, I was willing to make.

Not all sons and daughters will need distance and room from their parents in order to discover themselves in the midst and mist of adolescence. Not every parent will be willing to provide the space in any case, regardless of how badly or urgently the child might need it. These are individual choices that each family must make. Age is a guide, but in truth it is just a number. At some point in the very near future, prepare for your adolescent or teenage child to start to break away from you a little, and at some point very soon thereafter, you will have to learn to let go, a little.

FIVE THINGS
EVERY ADOLESCENT
SHOULD KNOW

※

There are many things an adolescent or teenager will need to know and understand in order to pursue a rich and purposeful life. Give your adolescent the basis of understanding who he is and he will become the very best version of the person he is meant to be. (As in many of these essays, "he" and "she" are used here interchangeably, instead of "he and she" or "he or she.")

Reward him for getting this far in his life, for surviving the mishaps and mayhem. He has earned it and deserves it. The five ideas that follow will provide him with some of the tools that he needs to survive, to thrive, to make the fewest mistakes, and to make the most of his opportunities. These are truths that can keep him out of trouble, keep him pursuing his greatest dreams, keep him in touch with the unique force of life within him, keep him out of bad relationships, and keep him pointed in the direction of his greatest passions and possibilities.

Provide him with the knowledge to understand the world around him, with context and texture, and you have given him the equivalent of compass points. How he uses them in his journey is for him to decide, but he will have truth and an unforgettable basis upon which to make his decisions.

1. KNOW RIGHT FROM WRONG

He has to know this difference. Whether he chooses to live by the knowledge or not is up to him, but he has to know it. Not because you tell him what is right from wrong, but because you live right from wrong. Your son watches everything that you do and studies you for habits, manners, methods, and skills to survive. Not unlike an eaglet whose eyes never leave the mother eagle—picking up her cues and knowledge until he is ready to fly from the nest. What you teach him, he will do. If he learns from you that truth is variable, depending upon the situation and who's telling the story, then he will not see the clear, clean line between right and wrong. If he learns from you that rules are bendable, depending on the circumstance and who needs what, he will not see that right and wrong are absolutes. He has to know the difference between the two in order to live a life of honor and respect.

2. KNOW PASSION

Passion is one of the most extraordinary of the emotions. It takes over and makes the simplest thing exciting and wonderful. Without passion, life is empty shadows with gray spaces in between. With it, life is a room full of friends watching the Super Bowl in HD. It is impossible to explain to a daughter what passion is. It would be as difficult as describing a bowl of vanilla ice cream on a hot summer day. The explanation cannot begin to compare to the reality. To know it is to feel it. You want your daughter to know what passion is, what it feels like, and what happens when it takes her over. But what is it?

Passion has no taste, smell, weight, color, dimension, or, in fact, any tangible properties whatsoever. Passion is a feeling only; it is purely emotion. So how do you teach her what it is? *You have to wait until it strikes her, and then embrace it completely.* Passion is the binding that ties your child to something in her life that she loves uncontrollably, illogically, unreasonably. It could be a singer, a song, a sport, a collection of dolls, a dream, or a cause. She may come to you effervescent about horses, stamps, the Beatles, a battle museum, or the Buffalo Bills. Whatever it is, it is her passion, at least momentarily. She has the right to know what passion feels and tastes like.

Passion is her everything.

For her to know it is her knowing her most basic self. Her passion is the instinctive guide she will use someday to find a job, choose a college, pursue a career, devote time to a charity, say yes to a great love, and live her own life. If you diminish or discourage her passion because it does not happen to be yours, you have taught her nothing. She is trying to find something that inspires her life, and she should know that she has your complete support and understanding of her pursuit, of her passion, *whatever* it is.

3 . KNOW CREATIVITY

"The path to self-respect is through creativity." So says Allee Willis, a very talented songwriter I know.

Creativity is a force within us. It is our innate and unique ability to see, hear, dream, and imagine things differently from how they are. Creativity is saying something that has never been said before. Creativity is thinking a thought that has never been thought before. It is imagining a melody or lyric or recipe or building that does not yet exist. Creativity is when we are most human. For our adolescents, creativity is when they are most themselves. Allow your child to discover his self-respect by recognizing and respecting and listening to his new ideas. By taking a few moments to listen and be patient as he explains his thoughts, you will provide him with a glimpse of a future where new ideas are worth something and every one has a place. His self-respect will grow from your respect of him. In a related story . . .

One of the greatest songwriters in the world, Mr. Lamont Dozier, tells the story of his being in third grade in a Detroit public school. His teacher, Mrs. Burke, would ask one student to write a poem on the blackboard one day, and the next day another student, and so on. When it was Lamont's turn, he wrote his poem, and Mrs. Burke left it on the board for a long time—almost three weeks, he remembers—because she liked it that much. Lamont had never known that kind of respect before, and sometime during those three weeks it occurred to him that maybe he was good at writing poems. This idea somehow grew in his head into the idea that he could be a songwriter if he wanted to. Mrs. Burke introduced him to his creativity, and he learned self-respect through being respected by her. She did a great thing, and the world would be a very different place without his writing the songs "Heat Wave," "Baby Love," "Where Did Our Love Go," "I Hear a Symphony," "My World Is Empty Without You," and thirty-four other number-one singles that defined a time in music known as the Motown era.

4. KNOW PERSPECTIVE

The fourth thing every adolescent should know is precisely and exactly where she is in the journey of her life. This knowledge underscores the importance of the decisions that she is making today that will long impact her future. So often children will make choices without considering the impact over a longer term than the next couple of weeks. Only much later do they wish they had chosen a different path. Former runaways will know exactly what this means, as will many high school dropouts. Perspective slows down the quick decision. Adolescents live for the moment, not for the future. Encourage a working knowledge of perspective by providing your child with your patience and understanding, your willingness to be truthful and honest about her chances of success in a particular venture, and your ability to look at both sides of an issue. Show how your life was affected by the decisions you made when you were in a similar place. Help your child understand that there is no joy in making an important decision in a vacuum, without considering all of the nuances, and that you can help if she needs you. It is her journey, but she has to know where she is on the map to her future. Provide her with perspective and she will never have to think about what she should have done or what might have been. There is no joy in realizing that your parents could have helped you but did not.

5. KNOW TRUST

The fifth thing every adolescent should know is what it feels like to be trusted. There is something so electrifying about the feeling, especially to an adolescent. Trusted to watch the house alone for a weekend, look after a younger sibling, hold on to the tickets to the football game, or entertain the boss for a few minutes while you go get the car. Even if it is something very simple, the very fact that people important in his life trusted him with something important in their life can be transforming. To be trusted is a harbinger of his oncoming adulthood and maturity, when he will be trusted more and more. To know trust is to know the foundations of love and loving. Without knowing how to trust someone, your child will never know how to open his heart to love someone. Love and trust are like water and air—without them both we are nothing. Let your adolescent know the feeling of trust and being trusted. Trust is the basis of friendship, peace, understanding, and almost every important relationship life offers. Let him know it first from you.

ORDINARY PEOPLE—
EXTRAORDINARY
PARENTS

※

There are many amazing parents out there who are raising their children with grace and dignity, and who are ushering into the world generation after generation of remarkable new young people. But the problem is that they are doing this in obscurity. No one notices. Nobody's recording it. There is no Parent of the Year award. There's no chance for the rest of us to learn from all of the excellent techniques they discovered in their parenting. It would be like Louis Pasteur never mentioning that he had figured out how to kill germs, or Thomas Edison keeping it to himself that he had created a lightbulb. That's almost what's happening right now. Great parents are creating great children and no one is keeping track of how they are doing it.

So, how about a television special? The Academy Awards for great parents. No negative exposés, or surprise cameras in unexpected places, or switching children from trailers to mansions. This show would be 100 percent positive and viewers would feel great when they watched. They would be inspired to be great parents too. Like the best of what *60 Minutes* does. Like the *CNN Heroes* show. The program would celebrate the world's greatest parents and describe in detail *how* they became the world's greatest parents. It would introduce the world to mothers and fathers who succeeded brilliantly with their children, who tried their best and got it right, who understood what was expected of them and met that challenge head-on. It would identify deserving people who discovered what sacrifice and compromise really mean and who deserve recognition for having accomplished something as remarkable as raising their amazing children, adolescents, or teenagers.

This show would highlight the stories of these parents, foster parents, teachers, elders, and coaches who had great ideas and followed through on them, clearly and definitively, without wavering from a course of respect, honor, encouragement, and patience. These are parents who chose to be kind, loving, encouraging, and respectful influences on their children's lives.

Maria Shriver could host. She would interview parents and ask them to describe in detail the rules and guidelines that they followed in bringing successful and principled young men and women into the world. The screen would flicker with amazing information, and the corresponding website would list these same ideas for parents at home who are watching the key milestones of their own adolescents' lives fly by like guardrails along the highway.

Cue music. Cue show logo. Off we go . . .

FIRST SEGMENT

Neil and Deborah. They have five children and, after more than twenty years of marriage, are still as dedicated to their relationship as the day they promised their hearts to each other. They are devout and patiently devoted to their family and to the community of families growing up around them. If you leave your child at their house after school, that child will get parented. He gets a snack, works on his homework, has to clean up after himself, and has no excuses for anything. Neil and Deborah are so good at parenting that they cannot help themselves. If I stay at their house too long, they start to parent me too. Theirs is the kind of family that you hope moves into the empty house across the street. You want their children to become best friends with your children. Under some very cozy lighting, Ms. Shriver would ask Neil and Deborah to share some of the guidelines that they used in raising their amazing children, and they would say something like this:

- You must love them "to pieces."
- You must show your love loudly and clearly, and frequently.
- You must show your love without conditions.
- Get your own life in order so you don't have to live through your children.
- When in doubt, trust them.
- Respect their privacy.
- You must not confuse who they are with who you want them to be.
- Encourage them to pursue the things they truly love—not necessarily the things they do well. The two are often not the same.

second segment

Just back from commercial, we meet Regina and Michael. She is an extraordinary parent, not only to her three re- markable children, but also to the thousands of children who attend the schools that she has presided over as assis- tant principal, after-school programs director, special-ed counselor, and head bottle-washer in her twenty-five years as an educator. She has partnered with me on all of my mentoring efforts at her school, the James A. Foshay Learn- ing Center, and she is cofounder with me of the Witness to a Dream Foundation. Maria Shriver would sit down with Regina and Michael and ask them what their keys to parenting amazing teenagers are. Regina would respond with these ideas:

- Be active and present in your children's lives every day.
- Keep your children actively involved in your life and in volunteerism.
- Keep your children so busy that there is not enough time for them to get into trouble.
- Children should be tired enough to sleep when they go to bed. If they are not tired, maybe they did not do enough that day.
- Parents should always be looking for parents with similar values, thus associating their own children with other children who have the same values.
- Consequences and punishments should be reduced if children tell the truth about what happened during their days' adventures.

THIRD SEGMENT

After station identification, we meet Genie, a manuscript librarian in the Special Collections Library at UCLA.

Maria Shriver would show up in an orange sundress to interview Genie, somewhere on campus, and these would be some of Genie's ideas for raising amazing teenagers:

- Always speak to them as equals. Never talk down to them or speak in overenunciated language when trying to get an important message across.
- Always encourage their exploration and discovery.
- Always make them tell you where they are and who they are with. Always.
- Always ask these questions before they leave the house: Where are you going? Who else will be there? How will you be getting home? What time will you be home? Do I know the parents?
- Chores are chores, and orders are orders. No cajoling. No pleading. They must do just what they have been told to do. Nothing move, nothing less.

For the final segment, Tom Brokaw would appear in a classroom surrounded by nervous and excited inner-city public school children and read the following: "Parenting is many gifts that we must learn to give. It is campaigns undertaken in quiet rooms with children who need nothing but love, and oftentimes more love than the parent, teacher, elder, or coach may have available at that particular moment. It is giving when there is nothing more to give. It is forgiving even when there is very little reason to forgive. It is knowing what to say and when to say it, and knowing when to say absolutely nothing. Parenting is allowing children to enjoy their lives, especially as adolescence dawns, illuminates, fractures, and complicates. What adolescents thought they knew about life and the world they live in changes from minute to minute and day to day.

"Parenting is helping adolescent and teenage children discover who they are, and who they are supposed to be and become. Parenting is helping them on their journey.

"Parenting is our greatest chance to make a real difference, to affect and impact the world around us, to repay our parents for their sacrifices on our behalf, to grasp an opportunity and make the most of it, and in so doing accomplish something really quite extraordinary—raising amazing adolescents and teenagers.

"On behalf of Maria Shriver and everyone else here at *Ordinary People—Extraordinary Parents*, this is Tom Brokaw. Good night."

It might never happen, but you've got to admit, that would be some show.

coming to terms
with what
might have been

In my earliest memories, I never remember a father. No Daddy-boy in my life at all. No Papa Bear. No familiar face of such a person on whom I could rely. I have searched, but there is no such presence in the pictures in my mind. My father passed away when I was just three. My mom tried to be both mother and father to me, but this did not always work out so well.

I remember when she wanted to show me how to throw a ball. Since she had never really tried before, and did not know how anyway, for many years I threw like a registered nurse. I saw a lizard in our yard once and tried to build a trap to catch it. She thought that just the sight of a lizard was a good reason to stop everything and smoke one of her unfiltered Chesterfields. Since there was never enough money, when we would shop for clothes, the guiding principal was that they had to be practical. All my pants and shirts were sizes too big and I always looked like I was shrinking.

I found myself looking around at the other boys and girls playing with their fathers, wondering what *that* was like. Big, strong people with deep voices and scratchy faces who could fix bikes and make everyone laugh and get tickets to baseball games. For little boys, growing up without a father is like growing up without one of your hands. You find a way to get through, but you notice that even the simplest tasks are so much easier for all of the other children. I never resented anyone, but I always wondered.

Whatever is missing or absent from his life can become quite present in a child's mind. Twins wonder about being only children, and an only child wonders what it would be like to have a sibling. Having an absent father makes a child wonder how having a father would change everything, while an overbearing parent gives a child cause to dream about a parent who is much less so.

It is very natural for adolescent or teenage children to compare themselves and their lives to those around them, and there is nothing wrong with it either. Even if you give your children everything, they will compare, they will wonder. Try not to take it personally when your daughter's remarks about her life seem to dismiss what *is* as she pines for or idealizes what is *not*.

The mere fact that I did not have a father does not mean that I cannot be a great father. The fact that I never had someone coach or mentor me does not mean that I cannot try to be a great coach or mentor. I have allowed the persistent longings caused by my father's absence to become a point of inspiration and to influence all my relationships with children, whether my own or those I teach or volunteer with or coach. It is a fact of my life that he is gone, and by trying to embrace that loss completely, I have endeavored to find my peace with it.

Parents of adolescents and teenagers, be inspired by what might be, not by what might have been. Be the greatest parent, whether or not you had great parents. Be the greatest coach, irrespective of your skills or abilities. Passion is a greater strength than heredity. Be the great enabler—allow your offspring to search for and discover who they truly are most meant to be. Your adolescent and teenage children deserve the best of you and what you have to offer them now, regardless of what happened long ago. If you have not been such a great parent until now, that does not mean you cannot be a great parent from now on. Even if you have yelled or hit, or caused your children unnecessary tears, you can stop that today too. If you have somehow stifled your child's big dream, you can find it and embrace it, and bring it back to life.

Today can be the first day of the rest of your parenting life.

once said,
never unsaid

❧

Adolescents are a remarkable cross section of the human experience. They are perched somewhere between childhood and adulthood, usually quite awkwardly, and nearly everything about them changes a little bit every day: faces and voices, big dreams, the quality of their understanding of the world around them, and even their sense of propriety and privacy. Each day they are wiser and know more than the day before. They understand this ever-changing version of themselves better with each passing weekend, and far better than their parents ever will.

Adolescents simply cannot wait to grow up. What's coming, what's coming, what's coming?—it's like a jungle drum beating up the silence. At this point in their lives, they are incredibly self-aware, self-conscious, self-everything. They are so excited about what is going to happen tomorrow that they can hardly wait for today to end.

Those of us who are privileged to be in the lives of adolescents must be very cognizant of the forces at play in the hearts and minds of these young people, and edit ourselves and our comments so that nothing we say could possibly injure their tender and growing egos, their burgeoning sense of appropriate and inappropriate, their formative years of attraction. The discovery of their inner beauty, their inquiries about life and love and the future, and their dreams of forever must be welcomed without hurried judgments and too-quick appraisals. We must show complete respect to them as people as they change and become someone else. We must be patient with them at all times, in all ways.

But here's the problem: If you ever do become unhinged for a moment or two and say something unkind to your adolescent child, you can *never* take it back. He or she will never let you forget it. Ever. Once said, it can never be unsaid. Save yourself the embarrassment and decades of apologies. Although I am sure that there are more, here are five phrases that should never be spoken to an adolescent or teenager:

1. "I DIDN'T RAISE MY DAUGHTER
   TO BE A . . ."

   Your daughter lives with you, she is in your care and under your wing, and hopefully trying to live within some edition of the moral and ethical framework that you have provided for her. This phrase, no matter how it ends, would not only hurt her but also be a harsh judgment of her life, her friends, her dreams, her everything. It is a hurtful accusation, suspicious, unkind, disrespectful, and diminishing.

2. "YOU ARE NOT GOING OUT OF THE HOUSE IN *THAT*."

By the time your daughter walks downstairs to show you what she has chosen to adorn herself with for a particular evening, whether going to a friend's house to study or to a party, it is likely that she has already gone through several different choices. She has thought about the pink or blue top, the red or black skirt, sleeveless or half-sleeves, the white or green or cream shoes, and so on down to the last detail. Her bedroom probably looks like Yves Saint Laurent's war room during Paris Fashion Week. Now, finally, with all of her creativity realized, and operating in full force, she has decided on the outfit in which she stands before you. She may look like Princess Diana, or she may look like Miss Long Beach, Queen of the Fleet. Or Miss Piggy. Who cares? Your first reaction must be a compliment. You must find something you like. You owe her this, particularly if you are the dad. This will be proof that you are accepting her changing beauty and allowing it to flourish. The clothes, the makeup, and the shoes are simply her creative whims come to gather. She carefully chose whatever it is, and if there is too much leg or arm or neck or décolletage, find the nicest possible way to let her know that she needs to make some adjustments. Try not to diminish or undermine her creativity and sense of self just because you do not agree with her sense of fashion.

3. "YOU'RE TURNING OUT JUST LIKE YOUR UNCLE NORMAN."

No matter how upset you are with your son, whether it is because of his clothes, his dirty shoes on your carpet, his grades, or how late he came home last night, never tell him that he is starting to remind you of someone else, that he is somehow not himself. If you suggest that he is, in fact, more like someone else than himself, especially someone you consider some version of a failure, it is a permanently demeaning thing to say. If ol' Uncle Norm is behind bars, or owes you some money, or has very bad table manners, or drinks like a fish, or whatever it is, you risk transferring some sliver of his identity and karma and juju to your son. Never say to your son that he is someone he is not: you may be damning him forever, linking his life to some unfortunate person who has nothing to do with him. By putting an actual portrait of an actual human being into your child's head, you will tattoo the features of someone else's failure on your child's face. You will complicate his adolescent life. Never tell your son who he is *just* like unless it is someone you love and adore and want him to be *more* like.

4. "YOU'LL NEVER BE ABLE TO . . ."

Any use of this phrase could easily derail a dream, disfigure a hope, write a tri-tone gap into life's melody, and in several other ways cause damage to an adolescent's unfolding. Imagine what it would be like to hear someone who is supposed to love you unconditionally and forever say, "You'll never be able to get into that great school . . . win the talent contest . . . write a hit song . . . become a veterinarian . . . be a model . . . live your beautiful dreams . . ." It is abject cruelty to tamper with an adolescent's possibilities. Let her try even if it seems impossible that she will succeed. The joy is the journey. Throw nothing in her path, least of all your doubts about her ability.

5. "I TOLD YOU SO."

There is no nice way to say "I told you so." Nor is there anything gained by saying it. This phrase is guaranteed to hurt somebody's feelings, no matter how it is said. It is mocking and judgmental and simply amplifies the magnitude of the failure, the good idea gone bad, or whatever it was that did not work. Imagine the son, humiliated already, near tears, walking up to his father, coach, or uncle, hoping for a little peace, love, and understanding, but instead finding someone who already has his hands on his hips, head shaking from side to side, lips pursed, mouth tsk-tsking him to even greater sadness. He is miserable and beating himself up already—what could be worse than a shower of "I told you so" raining down all around him. Not much.

Possibly no part of humanity is more sensitive to getting their feelings hurt than adolescents and teenagers. Peaches have more fortitude and resilience than that kid down the hall. Nothing hurts like words either. I'm not sure why this is, but it is. These young men and women, just breaking through the final few walls of childhood to get to adulthood, are listening to everything. They hear and remember every word that is said to them and about them.

Once said, never unsaid.

THE POWER OF
ONE BELIEVER

❧

Picture a sixteen-year-old boy. Six-foot-one and all of 160 pounds. Already way behind in the race to get a good education and go to a good college, have a good life, etc. Never heard of the SATs and never had a GPA. What's a GPA, anyway? Easily embarrassed and incredibly sensitive, smoked half a pack of Camel Lights every day. A big dreamer. A loner. Passionate and determined and absolutely certain that there was something more out there for him. He believed more than anything else that anything was possible. That was me.

I was back with my mom, in a tiny apartment in Laurel Canyon. She was starting over, too, and going to night school, so in addition to everything else, I was pretty much on my own, again. No one was looking out for me in the way a sixteen-year-old needs to be looked out for in the big-picture sense. I was unsure of how to talk about what had happened and tired of watching people react to the story with a look of "Huh?" on their faces. I just wanted to be normal for a while.

If a plot ever needed a twist, the story of my life did.

Out of nowhere, someone stepped up. Without being asked, without being assigned, without being requested, he somehow knew that he was needed. He elbowed his way into my life so gently that I hardly even knew he was there. He was Mr. Ernest Maria, father of my friends Joe and Vito. Mr. Maria started introducing me to people who he knew could help me. He would always say, "He's a good kid, he just needs a break." When the clutch on my '56 Chevy wore out, I mentioned to him that I had no money to get it repaired. He said he knew somebody. A couple of days later a mechanic called to say he could fix it for under $100. Yes, that's right, $100. It should have cost $1,000. When I needed a job, with no experience or résumé, Mr. Maria said that he knew somebody. He spoke with the man who owned the parking lot behind the Egyptian Theatre in Hollywood, and I got a $9-an-hour job parking cars there.

One day he asked me what I was going to do about school. I said I didn't know yet. He said he knew somebody. The next afternoon he brought me to Notre Dame High School, one of the best college prep schools in the city, which his son was attending, and introduced me to Brother Alphonso, the principal. Mr. Maria vouched for my character and said that he would be very appreciative if the school could find a seat for me. He even promised to pay my tuition if I faltered for some reason, which he knew (somehow) that I would never do. A couple of weeks later I was enrolled as a junior, without any transcripts of any kind, and no report cards to indicate where I had been. I was in my first legitimate educational setting since completing seventh grade three years before. All of this glory simply because some kind adult believed in me.

Mr. Maria pulled me back into the world and helped me find a place in line again. He looked after a fatherless boy he hardly knew, and changed the course and nature of the life that I was living. Mr. Maria was respectful, thoughtful, hardworking, dedicated to his family, kind to his employees, thankful for his beautiful wife, generous with his children, and he had a big enough heart to recognize that he was needed by a stranger, basically—and he had the courage to do something about it. He threw a little of his good luck my way. Because of him and a few simple kindnesses and introductions, my life changed forever. Without him, who knows what might have happened? It did not take much, but what a difference he made.

James, a New York–based lawyer, told me about growing up in a very poor section of Cleveland. He said that when he did something wrong as a child, he did not just get in trouble with his parents, he got in trouble with the whole *street*.

Everyone in the neighborhood knew that he had stolen a candy bar, gotten a bad grade, or been sent home from school with a note pinned to his chest. Neighbors would shout out at him as he walked home. Catcalls would splatter around him as he went by. "Why are you making trouble for your mother, son?" "Don't you have any sense of purpose in your life?" "She's not working hard enough to put food on your table, young man?" "Don't you dare turn out like that uncle of yours . . ." and so on.

The derision would cascade down on him like cold rain, shaming him, disgracing him, embarrassing him . . . and at the same time making him aware that these people believed in him and saw more in him. All of those neighbors formed a network in James's life, a network of believers. He turned out to be a good man who respects his family and his opportunities in life, who works harder than almost everybody else, and who has run his own big-city law firm for several years. He was lucky: His street was filled with prying eyes, caring strangers, and nosy neighbors who would not let him stumble his life away. He was ennobled by the power of the many people who believed in him.

⁂

Adolescence inspires distance between parents and children, and parents of adolescents can become very frustrated very easily. A conversation goes badly and the next one starts off just as badly. A pattern emerges and a widening gulf develops. A complicated issue becomes even more complicated. Sometimes the parents begin to resent the fact that their children do not appreciate all that has been done for them along the way. Sometimes the parents discover that their patience has simply run out.

But many adolescents still need someone, some thing, some act of kindness, some outside strength, some example of goodwill, some shoulder to cry on, some person willing to make a case for them, their decency, their inherent goodness. If that testimony has to come from outside the family, from outside the circle, from someone who is a new force in that adolescent's life, then so be it. One solution is to welcome the voices of outsiders in your adolescent's or teenager's life, the voices of other believers in his world. The voice could belong to a coach, a teacher, a neighbor, a best friend's mom, someone who can cut through the chatter and reach your child, make sense to him, inspire him in ways that you the parent cannot.

If a believer like Mr. Maria shows up in your son's or daughter's life, lucky you. Welcome him. Perhaps his experiences allow him to speak in a language that your adolescent will understand better than the language you speak. Maybe there is no water under the bridge. Maybe he can be more forgiving because he has not had to forgive as much. Perhaps he is a better listener because he has never had to listen, or he is simply willing to lend your child a hand, an offer of employment, a sense of purpose. Consider letting this happen.

At the same time, you may find yourself called upon to be a Mr. Maria to an adolescent or teenager in a corner of your life somewhere. She could be a niece, or a student, or an athlete you are coaching, or the kid next door. Possibly she cannot look up to her own mom or dad for whatever reason, but she sure can look up to you. Let her look up to you. Sometimes one small act can turn a life around completely. One conversation can reveal a long-hidden truth. One little flickering hope can obscure many lingering doubts. An ounce of faith can inspire an immeasurable amount of confidence.

There is a great power in being the one believer in an adolescent's life, and it is the power to change that life forever. And I can promise you this: There is no greater joy for an adolescent than when he or she finally finds that someone who really believes.

FOUR LITTLE
PHILOSOPHIES

꘏꘏꘏

While I am quick to recognize that there are many brilliant philosophers, and easily twice as many brilliant philosophies, I have also collected several that were never referenced in any Ralph Waldo Emerson collections. These help guide the way I parent and mentor and teach most all of the adolescents and teenagers I encounter in my life. Here are four of the best of those little philosophies.

1. LIFE IS LIKE A FOOTBALL GAME

Oddly enough, I got this one directly from a football player, Mr. John Matuzak, an enormous but philosophical man who played for the Oakland Raiders. He said that just like a football game, life moves forward, never backward. The clock is always ticking and the game is always progressing. You cannot go back and catch a ball you dropped or make a tackle you missed. You get that one chance and then it's time to get ready for the next chance. Here is how this philosophy applies: Take full advantage of every moment with your adolescent and teenage children. If you happen to make a mistake and lose your temper or otherwise show a complete lack of decorum, beg a little forgiveness and move on, and vice versa. If your child has disappointed you or otherwise left you dumbfounded by her actions, be ready to mumble some encouragement and move on to the next play. There is always a next play, another opportunity, a victory waiting just ahead. But there is no going back and trying it all again. At the end of our conversation, Mr. Matuzak wrapped his huge hand around my normal one. It looked like an octopus feasting on a strombus conch. He said, "One more thing, kid. Never let anyone diminish your self-respect—no matter what happened in the game."

2. THE QUINCY JONES RULE

After nearly sixty years of working with some of the most famous and well-known and controversial artists and writers in the world, winning countless Grammys and some Emmys, and being nominated for an Oscar and a Tony, Quincy Jones has never been dogged by a scandal. Not a one, and this is very unusual for a career in the music business. He has never been taken down for saying or doing something stupid that he could spend the rest of his life regretting. One of his philosophies is this: "Stay out of the head-lines and they can only judge you for your music." Here is how it applies: This little philosophy means that one should avoid the needless controversy that would be caused by some heartless comment or ac-tion. One should not speak out loud the unkind or critical remarks that dance across the mind as you attend your daughter's interpretive dance recital or listen to your son's first songwriting efforts. Per-haps try not to burst out laughing when your wife's sister falls on her @&% and throws the bean dip cas-serole halfway across the kitchen. Consider avoiding the bon mot that would send the room into fits of laughter but embarrass your son's coach. In other words, keep your mouth shut and they can judge you only for what you do best, which is hopefully your parenting.

3. THE ERIC LOWEN RULE

Years ago I worked for a publishing company and acquired the rights to a song called "We Belong." I gave the demo to Ron Fair, who gave it to Pat Bena-tar, who breathed big life into the lyric and melody with her recording of it, and had a big hit. Everyone made a lot of money, except me. The writers of the song were Eric Lowen and Dan Navarro, two wonderful and talented musicians. Not so long ago Eric called to say that he had contracted ALS, also known as Lou Gehrig's disease. I asked what that meant in practical terms and he said that they had given him a chart of what his next few years would be like: first a cane, then crutches, followed by a wheelchair, a motorized wheelchair, a tracheotomy, and near paralysis until death. There was nothing that he could do about it. Once it strikes, there is no cure. Eric, a father of five, singer, musician, songwriter, and all-around good guy, was soon going to be gone forever, just like that, with no options.

So out of respect to Eric Lowen and everyone else who has been taken down by this devastating disease, I try to live my life as if I have only those few years to live it in. I have no unnecessary arguments, no speeding through yellow lights, no unkindness in my life, ever. I try to show complete respect to everyone and anyone—from the guy parking the car to the lady getting me a caramel latte at the Starbucks. If I see someone who needs a hand, I stop and lend it. I help strangers cross streets. I write letters that get teenagers into great colleges with scholarships. Living by the Eric Lowen Rule has given urgency and momentum to my life, my career, my relationships, my mentoring, my coaching, and my parenting: I am always in a hurry to do the right thing and to do good things before I run out of time in which to do them, especially with my children. If you live your life as if you have only a few years to live, you will probably endeavor to leave a footprint different from that of someone who thinks he has all the time in the world.

4. THE JACKIE KENNEDY RULE

My mother and Jackie Kennedy had many similarities. Both of their lives were touched by great fortune and great tragedy, both were very young mothers whose husbands were taken from them under terrible circumstances, both lost a child in childbirth, and both were incredibly beautiful and brilliant women. They were also very close to the same age, and both died of cancer. My mother loved Jackie Kennedy, though she did not emulate her so much as admire and respect her completely. When Mrs. Kennedy once made an off-the-cuff remark about her parenting, it struck such a chord in my mother that she never forgot it. The words so perfectly summarized her own feelings on the subject, eloquently and unforgettably. Those words landed in my mom's heart like the seeds of roses finding refuge in soft soil somewhere. They grew and grew until they became her overriding philosophy when it came to the raising of her own children. It was simply this: "If you can't raise your children right, then what else is there?"

These four philosophies are, for me, reminders to be kinder, more loving, more supportive, understanding, patient, and willing. And to always try to be the best father I can be.

WHEN IT'S TIME, THROW THE BOX OFF THE ROOF

❧

There comes a moment in every adolescent child's life when his parents have to just stand back and see what is going to happen. After many years of prepping and preening, guiding and mentoring, the parents finally have to let their children loose in the world, out there *on their own*. Maybe it's a boy-girl party, or a class trip to Disneyland, or a summer of study far away. But it is the moment when parents have to trust that all of the work, time, effort, and guidance will have been enough. They have to hope and believe that they will be rewarded, that the child will be trustworthy and do the right things and make the right choices when given the opportunity to do so.

When this moment approached in my son Thomas's life, when he was about twelve or so and was invited to a party, without me, the importance of the forthcoming events was profoundly clear. Then—literally falling out of the sky—I saw something take place that made the significance of that moment so poignant and real, and that guided me in how to respond to his onrushing adolescence.

I was walking through the campus of Grandview Elementary School, the public school that both of my sons attended. I happened to be there on the day that one of the great traditions of that school was being enacted. It is an experience that all Grandview second-graders are asked to participate in, an experiment in creativity, planning, design, cause and effect, imagination, and responsibility. The students are asked to build a box that will hold an egg and protect that egg under very difficult circumstances. The box can be made out of any material, but the students are asked to limit themselves to normal items found around the house. I was walking by at just the right time. All of the boxes had been built and submitted and filled with eggs, and Mr. Jim, the school's custodian, had taken several trips up a ladder to the roof of a one-story building that housed all of the second-grade classrooms. Once everyone was ready and everything was in place, he started to throw the boxes off the roof. What a sight it was! In every color, shape, and configuration, enormous cardboard raindrops tumbled down out of the sky. Each one hurtled to the grass below. For a brief moment, each box was suspended in air—working perfectly to protect its precious cargo. But then, *boom-boom-boom*, they started to land. Each with its own unique thud. Children and parents gasped and twitched and oohed and aahed. When the last box hit the ground, there was a brief moment of silence, and then, on a signal from their teachers, all of the students rushed to retrieve their boxes to see what had happened to the eggs. I must say that many more eggs survived than I had thought, but just as many did not. Some had only a tiny crack in the shell, and others looked like they had right then dropped out of the hen.

As I watched, it occurred to me that this experiment was very much like the journey we were about to take with Thomas. He was the egg, precious and perfect, practically unmarked by life so far. The box was all that Antonina and I had done to prepare him for life and what could happen, all our wisdom and genius and insight and prayers. The flight and the landing was going to be the most difficult part, the actual adolescent and teenage years that were about to begin.

We fill the corners of their little boxes with scraps of our decency, our kindness, our torn shreds of knowledge, balled-up cautions, and long-held truths. We fret and worry and carefully wrap these things in all of the genius we ever were able to find in our own lives. We do all of that and then hope and pray that everything will turn out okay. Possibly, and maybe, if we pack and prepare and do everything just perfectly, when the box lands everything will be fine. But not always will we be so lucky, and some eggs will crack a little. Others will land funny and will be almost ruined by their brief flight and sudden fall to earth. Once the box is in the air, anything can happen. Once adolescence begins, anything can happen.

Life is what happens to us. Part of life is that journey from the roof to the earth. Children must survive their adolescent and teenage years just as they somehow survived everything that came before, whether being one of two million or so tiny spermatozoa, somehow finding a place in that egg, then nine months of gestation, the risks of birth, all those inoculations, the big boo-boo, first days at school, learning to be friends with new children, growing up, getting in trouble, missing an open goal or basket in an important game, and all the other millions of thresholds of childhood that will define them.

Adolescence and teenage years are just one of many rites of passage. We are there to guide and mentor, to protect and defend, to try to keep them from hurting themselves or being hurt by life. But at a certain point, we can only watch and see what happens when life happens. When it's time, be fearless. Like diving in a pool for the first time. Just close your eyes and let go. When it's time, just throw the box off the roof.

PART TWO

GROW THE TREE
YOU GOT

G row the Tree You Got" is one of the essays in my first book, *Parking Lot Rules & 75 Other Ideas for Raising Amazing Children.* It was one of the most popular and often discussed essays that I was able to carve out. While this applies to children, it is even more important for adolescents and teenagers to be individually appreciated for who, what, why, and how they are as people.

One of the greatest responsibilities we have as parents is to help our children discover themselves, discover exactly who and what they are supposed to be, and help them grow into their own skin while teaching them that it is okay to become whoever they turn out to be. We are expected to provide guidance, mentoring, direction, and wisdom. But we are also expected to assist the person inside them to find a way out without getting ruined along the way. Not easy.

Here follow some ideas on how to give and get the most out of your relationships with the adolescents and teenagers in your life, while allowing them to discover and become themselves.

ROCKS IN THE ROOTS

❧

During windstorms and hurricanes, big trees often get top-
pled over. Arborists use this opportunity to study the root
systems of the big trees. The scientists are looking for an
understanding of how a tree established its footing in the
earth, that particular tree's journey from seed in dirt to tow-
ering elm or birch or pine. One of the most interesting finds
when examining the roots of a downed tree is the frequent
discovery of an enormous rock or rock field deep within its
root system. The tree would appear to have encountered
the rock very early in its life, overcome the obstacle that the
rock represented, and ultimately turned the rock into a part
of its strength and foundation.

Based on the fact that the rocks are often so close to the
surface, arborists surmise that the tree must have been very
young when it met the enormous and nearly overwhelming
obstacle represented by the rock. The tree's root system was
likely still in the developmental phase, still establishing

itself in the earth. The tree had to conquer the rock, or at least make peace with it, and turn its negatives into the tree's benefits and positives. It had to make adjustments or risk its survival. The rock must have seemed an overwhelming challenge to a tree just a few weeks or months old. Cold, unforgiving, and so much bigger and stronger than the sapling's tiny roots as they trembled in the terra firma, searching for water and nutrients and a way around a huge problem.

But the tree had its destiny, too; it had business to accomplish, a reason to be there, a life to lead. The tree had to find a way to turn disadvantage into advantage, imbalance into fulcrum, weakness into strength, the impossible into the future. Despite the enormity of the challenge, rocks are key to a tree's ultimate survival because they retain moisture and water with greater efficiency than the soil. Without them, the tree would have less of a chance to grow and thrive. By overcoming them, the tree makes itself that much stronger.

There may be a moment in your own adolescent's or teenager's life when he comes face-to-face with something incredibly difficult. Something that at first dwarfs his resolve, that outweighs his courage 100 to 1, that is insurmountable in every respect. It might be social, educational, physical, or emotional. It might be a sickness, an accident, or an unkind remark from an unexpected place. It might be the loss of a close friend or the failure of a big dream. It might be a bad coach or getting kicked off a team. Just like the little tree, alone, trying to find its way through the cold soil of youth and adolescence to its adulthood, your child may find himself desperate and outnumbered, in circumstances beyond his control, with knowledge and wisdom in short supply, his resolve and passion dwindling. More than likely, you will not know much about the crisis, as it will be happening there beneath him, in the darkness, where his roots are extending into the world.

If your beautiful little sapling runs into a rock, that is the time when your nurturing is most needed, your kindness and understanding is most wanted, your encouragement and faith in him is most necessary. The sunlight and water, hope and belief, that you provide may be the only relief or nutrients that he is going to find. Your love may be what he needs most to survive and conquer this challenge.

But he, not you, has to figure out how to get past the big rock. He has to get by it, or through it, or around it, somehow, and get on with his life in spite of it. He has to wrestle with his issues, whatever they are. He has to turn this obstacle into an advantage. You can support and encourage, but he has to go through it. What may seem impossible for your son to overcome today may well be the rock he uses to balance on to build the foundation of his life tomorrow. Be understanding. Be loving. Be supportive. Be sunlight. Be nourishment. Be moisture. Be whatever your son needs. Help him overcome whatever it is that has gotten in his way, whatever it is that has impeded his progress. Encourage and enable him to turn the rocks in his way into rocks in his roots.

TWELVE SWING THOUGHTS

Golf is a humbling game. It teaches you everything that you might ever want to know about yourself, and then some. Even if you do not want to know that particular thing about yourself, golf will teach you anyway. Find out how you deal with triumph, tragedy, fury, and exultation, and that's just on the first hole. There are eighteen holes in a round of golf, and each is a unique test of valor and will, patience and skill.

In most sports, a foul is a foul only when you get caught doing it, and if you don't get caught, it isn't a foul. Not so in golf. It is the only game I know where participants call their own fouls and mistakes and announce them to the other players. The rules are the rules. If a ball goes out of bounds, it goes out of bounds. If you hit another player's ball, you lose the hole. If you turn in the wrong score, you are disqualified. An honorable and ancient game, to be sure. But what golf is really all about is the swing. You have to get that right or you have nothing.

The swing is the essence of the game. It is what happens during those few frantic seconds when a player tries to connect fantasy to reality by making the ball fly up in the air exactly as he imagines it will. The swing is one of the most difficult things to learn *how* to do, and one of the easiest things to *forget* how to do. For this reason, when someone is taught how to play the game, the teacher will usually provide some tools to help him or her remember what the swing is all about.

These are called "swing thoughts."

By necessity, swing thoughts must be simple and easy to remember, as they will be the very last thing that races through a player's mind before he confidently draws back his club and hits the ball right into a lake. Or into the trees. Or misses it completely. Or, on the rare occasion, hits it perfectly, right at the hole.

Here are some examples of good swing thoughts: "Finish with the hands high." "Keep your head down." "Get your hips through the ball." "Let the club do the work." "Roll the rock, baby." And so on. A good swing thought should be based on a positive idea, a seed of hope, an expression of possibility, a complete faith in the outcome. A swing thought should never begin with a negative. A negative swing thought will taint the swing and suggest to the golfer the possibility or likelihood of a mistake occurring. A negative swing thought is often a harbinger of a bad swing. I have heard players fill their heads with bad swing thoughts, and then fulfill the promises hidden therein. They stand over the ball and say very mean things to themselves. Like: "Don't chunk it, you ignoramus." "No slicing, no slicing . . ." "Try not to hook it this time, fathead." "Do not hit it thin. . . . Do not hit it thin!" "Just keep it out of the sand, you know you can't play out of the sand." "Not in the water, Oprah, not in the water!"

The result of these bad swing thoughts, more often than not, is that exactly what the player does *not* want to happen happens, sometimes followed by some terrible language and occasionally by the tossing of expensive clubs into deep canyons. It would be hard to do anything well with a head full of negative thoughts. Positive thoughts are much more effective. In golf and in raising amazing adolescents and teenagers.

Imagine that the adolescents in the next room are like new golfers and you are their teacher. If you give them swing thoughts that are positive and encouraging and possible to achieve, they just may respond in kind. If you give them swing thoughts that are kind and helpful, that fill their hearts with hope, that encourage and inspire, they just may begin to believe that they can achieve anything. Such as run for class president, or apply to study overseas, or speak to the principal about an important issue, or take a big test, or stand up to an unkind friend, or play piano in a big recital, or even hit a golf ball. To get your adolescents and teenagers in the habit of thinking of themselves in the most positive way possible, parents should try to speak to them in the most positive way possible. Turn negative thoughts into positive ones.

NEGATIVE THOUGHT	POSITIVE THOUGHT
Don't be mean to your sister.	Be kinder to your sister, please.
Stop throwing things in the house.	I'll get my glove . . . let's go play catch.
Do *not* get in trouble today.	Make me proud of you today.
Stop being so rude to Grandma.	Let's be extra nice to Grandma.
Why are you being a smart ***?	There must be a better way to say that.
You'd better not be lying to me.	The truth reduces the punishment by 90 percent.

Like a golfer standing over an important shot in a big tournament, your daughter may someday soon find herself in need of a great swing thought, a touch of your wisdom to consider right before plunging into something enormous and challenging. The swing thought that you offer her now may be precisely the idea that she searches for (and finds!) just before a key moment later in her life. If she is applying to a great school, or being interviewed for a prized scholarship, or competing for a key summer internship, think of the peace and simple pleasure she will enjoy when she hears your voice in her head, saying something incredibly positive to her, encouraging her, believing in her, supporting her, now and always. She might just get a quiet rush of confidence remembering how you always used to give her such great swing thoughts when she was younger and life was simpler. Possibly like these:

You can do anything.

I believe in you completely.

Give all you can give—that's all that matters.

Play like a champion today. (Notre Dame football motto)

Butterflies are proof you're competing.
  (Michael Jordan)

Be brave for the first minute, then everything will take care of itself.

In chaos there is great opportunity. (Napoleon)

Life is what happens.

I have faith in you, and trust you.

I am so glad you turned out to be you.

Try your hardest—that's all you can do.

You *can* do this.

FATHERS AND DAUGHTERS

A father's relationship with his daughter is the most important relationship that she will have in her life. It is, in my opinion, the basis and template for all the relationships that she will have with all the men in her life. Teachers, coaches, boyfriends, bosses, fathers-in-law, sons, and grandsons. What she knows from her relationship with her father is what she will think love is.

If her father is unkind and unforgiving, she may think that love is harsh.

If her father interrupts her when she speaks and never listens to her whole answer, she may think that love is impatient and hurried.

If her father is stingy with his compliments and gratuitous with his criticism, she will think that love means judging someone.

If her father raises his voice to her, and shouts her down, she could believe that love is intimidation and intimidating.

If her father ever calls her a name other than her own, especially when he is upset with her, she would have reason to think that loving someone can mean ridiculing them.

If her father is any of these kinds of men, he may turn around one day and notice that all his daughter's boyfriends and husbands were obnoxious and disrespectful jerks. When he says to her, "What did you ever see in those guys?" she will have every right to say, "You, Daddy."

If her father is any of these kinds of men, when he visits his daughter at her office years from now and notices that her boss is a temperamental and fractious man, difficult to read and impossible to please, he may say, "Why do you work for this guy . . . ?" She may say, "He reminds me of you, Dad."

If a father is any of these kinds of men, he may never even bother to notice that he is doing his daughter any harm at all. He may choose to remain blissfully ignorant of the impact his actions may be having. But a father who limits the ways that love and joy and trust enter his young daughter's heart limits the ways she can love later in her life. By providing her with kindess and respect and happiness when she is growing up, he will allow her the freedom to love when she is grown. A father with high expectations of his daughter is very different from one who is impossible to please. A father who is firm with his daughter is very different from one who is unkind or mean to her. A father who encourages her dreams is very different from the father who is overly practical and analytical about her future. A father who learns to trust his daughter's instincts is very different from the man who is suspicious of her intuition and, in turn, her choices and friends. A father with the ability to listen to his daughter when she wants to speak with him—and the ability to understand why when she does not—is very different from the man who is intolerant of her changing moods and frustrated by her inconsistency.

But she will become accustomed to him, whoever her father is. His habits and nuances and subtleties in the way he loves her and treats her will be the basis of many of her relationships with men. Her father is her first great love. Learning to love him and live with him will provide the foundation of how to love and live with all the men who will be in her life.

THE SEVEN BRIDGES RULE

By the time Thomas was twelve, I thought that I had built many bridges between us. I believed, very naively it turned out, that there were plenty of connections that we could use to get to one another. I was married to his mother, we all lived in the same house, I was his soccer and basketball coach, we went to see every new movie and the occasional rock concert, and we always had our annual ski trip to plan and execute. But when his adolescence arrived, everything changed, and oh boy, did it change. Not just because of him and the hormones and all of that business, but because the roof caved in. First, he decided he did not want to play soccer anymore; he wanted to play football. When I reminded him of how good he was and of the investment of time he had made developing his skills, he turned to me and said, "I'm done with it, Dad. That's it." A bridge between us that had lasted for seven years, through twelve different uniforms and countless evenings and hundreds of games and practices, was suddenly gone.

Then, a few months or so later, he told me that he wanted to start seeing movies with his friends, not with his dad all the time. (Yes, this is the same story as appears earlier in the discussion of Learning to Let Go, a Little.) That particular bridge between us was built when he was just four and we saw the film *Babe* twelve Saturdays in a row ("That'll do, pig, that'll do . . ." became a long-standing catchphrase between us). Over that bridge had walked every new film that was worth seeing in addition to a scene-by-scene breakdown of films like *Jurassic Park* and *Star Wars* plus the entire Preston Sturges catalog as well. Two bridges were down.

Shortly after that, he discovered that he liked only hip-hop music, not the rock and roll that Dad liked so much. To heck with U2 and Bon Jovi concerts—the music that I loved and wanted to share with him was suddenly old-fashioned and boring. Bridge number three was suddenly out of commission now too.

Then the equivalent of the Golden Gate Bridge fell into the ocean. At this critical juncture in my life with my son, with everything between us changing, suddenly everything changed. His mother and I separated. Our marriage was over and just as suddenly as that, Thomas and I did not even live together anymore. All that was left of bridge number four were some pilings. My whole game plan to be one of the greatest fathers ever was under siege and at risk of complete failure. I wanted to give Thomas what I did *not* have, not re-create the sitcom that was my adolescence. I wanted him to have both parents—living together with him in the same house that he had grown up in, in a little town somewhere. But more than anything else, I wanted him to grow up with a dad in his house. By trying to make his life near-perfect, possibly I could make mine just a little less imperfect. That was the plan anyway.

The key to success is to do the things that you are supposed to do *when* you are supposed to do them. Not later, not tomorrow, but right now, right when they are supposed to get done. I used this guideline as my touchstone during this period. The challenge I gave myself was to continue to be the greatest father I could possibly be, even though Thomas and I did not live together anymore. Where is my son? What is he doing? Who is he with? became very persistent questions that rained down on me like it was just another day in Seattle. These became my first thoughts every day. It was not an easy thing to do but I saw that I had no other choice, and as a result I was always available to him and he saw me every day. I would drive him to school every morning until the day he got his driver's license, and some days those few minutes were all the time we had together that day.

In the midst of all of the other things going on, such as

life, and a career, and a new house, and a new relationship, I started to build new bridges between Thomas and me. I also tried to rebuild the old bridges between us that still had a chance. I had to discover and rediscover what the new, adolescent version of him liked to do, what the new version of him liked to eat, how the new version of him wanted to spend time. Most important for me to discover was what the new version of him loved more than anything else in the world (which turned out to be music!). I continued to reach out to him constantly, but it was not easy fighting adolescence and teenager angst while I was living somewhere else. Although there was less of a dominant male figure in his life, this gave him a little more room to discover what he wanted to do with his life and how he was going to start making that life happen.

Before adolescence hits, think to build seven strong bridges between you and the adolescent or teenage child in your life. These bridges represent anything that you share or enjoy together, that you can love together, that you can have together . . . dreams, hobbies, practices, aversions, tasks, volunteer projects, even a sports team. These bridges must be built with care, treasured, valued, constantly kept up. Whether emotional, intellectual, or involving passions, bridges between you and your teenagers can provide transport for the vital building blocks of a good relationship.

Always look for a good bridge, as one can show up un-expectedly and suddenly. Your son's new dream can be the start of a new bridge as long as you are willing to join him in pursuing it. Let's say that, thanks to Guitar Hero, he has become a huge fan of Steely Dan or some other band you forgot existed. Dust off the leather jacket, adjust the toupee, find the old Doc Martens, and take him to a show—an amazing bridge-building opportunity. If your daughter dis-covers that she loves animals and suddenly wants to volun-teer at an animal shelter every Saturday afternoon, you can go along with her. It could be a great bridge between you. It does not have to be your joy that you are introducing her to, and it is not just your passion that you are teach-ing her to pursue. Possibly your adolescent's joy or passion can be the start of the next bridge to span the distance be-tween you. Obviously, you have to put your child first to make any of this work.

Start building your bridges now, early—many seasons in advance—and be ready to build new ones the moment one of the old ones gives out on you and starts to crumble into the river of adolescence rushing below. Here are some pos-sibilities on which to build seven bridges between you and the adolescent in your life:

1. A hobby you pursue, together.
2. A team you root for, together.
3. A sport you play, together.

4. A religious or cultural tradition you practice or preach, together.
5. A regularly scheduled trip you take, together.
6. An afternoon's distraction you can enjoy, together, like a museum or a local fair.
7. An act of volunteerism that you do, together.

The key to the success of any of these bridges is that you be *together* with the adolescent or teenager in your life. Not necessarily physically together, however, but being together is what makes it a bridge between you. You both have to be involved and present in the same moment, pursuing the same goal, dream, laugh, or purpose.

I am pleased to report that as of this writing, Thomas has discovered his passions in music and writing and he believes that both will be important parts of his future. He has a backpack full of big dreams that he hopes to accomplish in his lifetime. He has helped me rebuild some of the bridges that were washed out years and years ago as well. I coached him to two more basketball championships when he was in high school, a new bridge. I made sure he got a car. I introduced him to some of my clients whose music he loved, another bridge. I became less and less his overly precious father, and more his patient enabler. This became a bridge of understanding between us. But most important to me, because I never gave up on the relationship between us, he realized that I loved him and had never left him. His adolescence was not the perfect thing I imagined it would be, but it was nowhere near as imperfect as it might have been.

Bridges will come and go; some will fall apart and be rebuilt, others will disappear forever. But what travels across them never changes: it is the love, kindness, friendship, and respect that are so vital to a successful relationship with a son or daughter.

WORST-CASE-SCENARIO SYNDROME

❧

After many years as a parent, I have discovered that I suffer from a syndrome. It's called Worst-Case-Scenario Syndrome. Or WCSS: it rhymes with "fix."

Symptoms include sweaty palms, facial tics, gritting and grinding teeth, and excessive heartburn. WCSS most often strikes parents of adolescent and teenage children. Sufferers imagine the very worst possible thing that could happen, and then just dwell on it. Could be hours, or days. Whatever news they are given, or questions they are asked, parents cannot help themselves. Sweat runs down their backs, their hands get clammy, maybe a few spots start to cloud their vision, and then all they can imagine is that something terrible is happening somewhere, somehow, with, for, or because of their child. Parents with WCSS lead nervous lives. A text comes in from a daughter that starts out, "We need to talk . . ." and suddenly there's not enough air in the universe. A son tweets, "You're not going to believe what just happened . . ." and WCSS parents' faces squint like ceremonial Pygmy hunting masks. The phone rings at an odd hour and they put the cat in the dishwasher. Although there is no official count, I bet WCSS attacks occur more often than the Fox network runs commercials for NASCAR, if that is even possible.

Here is a scenario frequently discussed at WCSS support groups in towns all over America: Your son calls to say that he "misplaced" the credit card you let him use for ten minutes to buy a new video game. This call immediately triggers a WCSS attack. You imagine your digital identity already stolen, the thief on his way to Mazatlán in a first-class seat, covered in loud and tasteless, but very expensive, jewelry you paid for. His new Gucci bags are filled with scuba gear courtesy of your son and your maxed-out credit card. Blood pressure rises, breathing is strained, and you pinch a pressure point in your forearm to reduce the nausea. Just as you are about to let your son have a piece of what is left of your mind, he texts you to say that he found the card, it was in the other pocket. Barely breathing, you remark to the sugar bowl, "Oh, he found the card, what great news. Who would have thought to look in the other pocket?" For the next hour or so you are as jumpy as a bail bondsman in New Orleans on New Year's Eve. But that's okay. It's nothing to worry about. You're just WCSS-ing.

.   .   .

Worst-Case-Scenario Syndrome can create absolute panic in many parents' fragile and delicate hearts. A little bit of potentially bad news sends a tumbler of adrenaline squirting into the bloodstream and for hours sufferers have to try to get over it. After a few episodes of WCSS, parents begin to hope that they may someday grow accustomed to the increased heart rate, flustered and fluttering hands, and gray hairs popping out everywhere, especially in or about the ear area. Suddenly they understand their own parents so much better. I have suffered from Worst-Case-Scenario Syndrome for many years now. I can honestly say it has led me absolutely nowhere—nowhere good, anyway. WCSS-ing is the starting point for long-remembered bouts of panic, doubt, paranoia, dread, and lots of other feelings I would rather not admit to having as a grown man of a certain age. Thomas and Sam have much better things to do with their days than help me manage an overactive imagination and correspondingly overzealous adrenal glands.

I try to recognize that my view is completely skewed the moment my WCSS kicks in and discount my own catastrophic thoughts accordingly. I have come to understand that my judgment is nearly worthless at these moments and that I rush to unkind conclusions when in the throes of an attack. On top of that, I am surprisingly capable of saying things that only ratchet up the angst of everyone involved.

So in the interest of keeping things safe and sane, I try to take a big step back from the edge when WCSS strikes.

Experts in the field opine that WCSS is absolutely normal for parents of adolescents and teenagers and almost nothing can be done to prevent it. It goes away gradually, like pimples, and your hairline. Adolescents become teenagers and teenagers become young adults and responsible for themselves more and more, and the WCSS-ing reduces in both frequency and intensity. These same experts did recommend that in the meanwhile I might take more naps, drink decaffeinated coffee, purchase a lucky rabbit's foot, acquire a set of worry beads, and hang some horseshoes upside down above the kitchen door. Just knowing WCSS exists has saved me a lot of time and agony, and kept me from being sophomorically and ridiculously unkind to my children when I've felt another attack coming on.

DISAPPOINTMENT
AND PERSPECTIVE

❧

Some Saturdays ago, at a local soccer field, a woman who I knew from the neighborhood approached me and said, "So you wrote that book . . . ? That one about children . . . ? Did you happen to write anything about how to deal with my completely rude and disrespectful teenage daughter?" The look on her face said everything her words did not, and matched the tone of her voice perfectly. She was U-P-S-E-T. Her husband was sitting nearby. He joined in: "I can hardly wait for this part to be over. I'm not even talking to this girl right now."

Their daughter was fifteen, athletic, proud, unbending— all life skills that girls need to get anywhere in this world these days. The parents described the essence of the problem: the incredibly rude way the girl spoke to the adults in her life. As an example, the mother told me about a soccer game the day before in which the daughter was given a red card (i.e., thrown out of the game) because of the way she kept challenging one of the referee's calls. Apparently she told the center ref that he was having trouble with his calls because he did not bring his guide dog. On the ride home, already embarrassed by her daughter's actions, the mother punished her further by taking away her phone and several other privileges. Both parents were so irritated with her in general that everything and anything easily sparked a new wave of anger. Already antagonized, they were easy to outrage. The mother was a lioness with a thorn in her paw.

Like an ornithologist who will always find a moment to talk about owls, I can always find a moment to talk about children, adolescents, or teenagers. I asked them if I could ask them a few simple questions about their daughter.

Q: "Is she taking drugs or drinking?"

A: "No."

Q: "Is she involved in a relationship with a boy or a friend that you are not happy about?"

A: "No."

Q: "Is she a good student?"

A: "Yes, excellent."

Q: "Is she a good athlete?"

A: "Yes, absolutely."

Q: "Do you like her friends?"

A: "Yes."

Q: "Is she a good sister and, other than the way she
   speaks sometimes, a good daughter?"
A: "Yes, yes, yes . . . She's just so rude!"

I thought to myself: "She sounds pretty cool to me." I
began to wonder what the problem was. Loving parents, a
great child, a stable home and family, but people were not
getting along as they should. Made no sense.

⁂

The day before the conversation above took place, I was at
the James A. Foshay Learning Center in South Los Angeles, six miles away but a whole different universe. Music
is a part of my mentoring program and I was conducting a
choir rehearsal. Three ninth-grade girls were waiting to audition, ready to sing a cappella in front of the whole choir.
Two of the girls were cousins who sang in perfect harmony,
and they got right in. But the third girl was not in very good
shape. Within a couple of feet, you could smell alcohol on
her breath. Her eyes were half closed. She was woozy and
off balance—possibly experiencing morning sickness, the
assistant principal whispered to me. She looked like she had
as much chance of succeeding at life as I had at joining the
Lakers. Even the possibility of graduating from high school
was looking slim. Her image flashed before me as I was
speaking to the parents on the soccer field.

I could not help thinking that she had probably never known a parent who cared for her patiently and consistently. She had probably never known a protector and defender of her morals and her intellect. She likely had no one telling her to try harder, reach higher, achieve greatness, and try to have a better life than the one she was having. I could not help thinking what she must have gone through already and would probably have to go through in the days and months and years ahead.

This girl and my neighbors' soccer-playing daughter were the same age, in the same grade. Both had started at the same time, roughly, and though they lived only a few miles apart, they may as well have been on different continents. One was practically lost already, while the other was just having a difficult couple of months. One had made several bad choices and was living with the consequences, while the other was just a smart aleck. One was likely to be dependent on the system during her whole existence, while the other had a life path opening before her that almost anyone would want. One had stumbled so many times already that her family had apparently written her off, while the other had a dedicated family structure there to catch her if she ever did fall, which looked pretty unlikely. An embarrassment of riches versus a wealth of opportunities lost.

The gulf that separated these two girls was immense. The parents of the straight-A, superbly athletic, slightly rude girl agreed when I shared some of the details of the straight-D, out-of-shape, perhaps intoxicated, maybe pregnant inner-city ninth-grader's life. Their daughter was amazing, and she needed to make only a few tiny corrections. She was like a vintage Porsche with a squeaky brake, i.e., almost perfect. But it seemed that her parents had run out of patience *as parents*. They were so irritated by the experience of getting their daughter through a difficult period that they were angry before any conversation even began. The problem was manifested in the way the parents and their daughter were interacting with each other. In the words of the prison warden in *Cool Hand Luke*, what we had here was a failure to communicate. Nothing more than that.

So I made two recommendations for the parents. First was that whenever they spoke to their daughter, they did so in the most kind and respectful way they possibly could. No more frustrated or angry tones, no more raised voices, no more threats, only kindness for a while. If they did get upset, they had to whisper—like it was a law. "When we get upset, we whisper?" the mother asked, incredulous. Their daughter was already so sure they would be upset with her that she was going into every conversation on the defensive, protecting herself, always ready to fight back. Not such a bad skill set to have, when you think about it.

Second, I told them it was necessary to show their daughter how much they loved her while at the same time requesting that she change her behavior. How do you show or measure something as intangible as love? I took a quarter out of my pocket and handed it to the mother and said, "You can use this coin to help everyone in the conversation gain perspective. Tell your daughter that you love her as much as this whole soccer field, but that you are *upset* with her only the size of the quarter. Ask her if she can help you fix the part represented by the quarter." It was a way to put the problem and disappointment into an easily understood perspective.

They agreed to try out these two ideas out and we promised to speak again soon.

A couple of weeks went by and I ran into the mother at the local Coffee Bean. I asked how everything was going with her daughter. The smile that broke out over her face was so beautiful and bright as she described a tea they had enjoyed the day before, an upcoming spa trip, the family's plans for Christmas, and so on. She said, "When I stopped speaking to her in a mean voice, she stopped answering me in a mean voice, and everything changed. She stopped being so difficult." She said that the quarter helped give the context needed for the necessary corrections in her daughter's communications with the adults in her life. The mother concluded, "Things are not perfect, but they are a lot better, and who knows, they might get perfect at some point soon."

Disappointment is all a matter of context. When it comes to our own adolescents, we set higher standards for them than the rest of the world does. We expect more from them because we are completely invested in them and their future. When dealing with an adolescent who has disappointed her parents, the greatest level of patience and kindness and perspective is required. Maybe it is not the end of the world after all. Maybe a daughter just cannot find her "polite" button. She is still owed understanding, respect, support, and the very best her parents have to offer. Perhaps she has done things that are infuriating, antagonizing, and impossibly rude as well. Did she set out to ruin everyone's day? Was it intentional? Or was it just her natural defense mechanisms, her growing up, her sharpening sense of self, her instinct come to life? Parents need to decide before they criticize. Adolescents and teenagers usually outgrow their bad habits if pressured with patience.

Some of the traits of an adolescent child that are most annoying may be just the traits that save her later in life. Take the daughter with the smart mouth who is not afraid to talk back to anyone, whether at a soccer game or a scolding from her father. Imagine her ten years from now, being bullied to drink too much at a party, or with a boyfriend who is trying to advance a relationship before she is ready. Won't that smart mouth come in handy? Won't her ability to talk back be just the tool she needs to defend herself? Won't a little rudeness be very practical? Her refusal to keep quiet and just go along may have a huge value in a difficult situation.

At the same time, disappointment is as much a part of raising amazing adolescents and teenagers as pride and elation. Disappointment is really just a measurement: the difference between what you expect of your child and what she delivers. Disappointment is the distance between what you hope she will do and what she actually does. Today's disappointment can be tomorrow's defense. Today's rudeness can be tomorrow's career path. Today's obnoxious daughter can become tomorrow's president of her own company. Be careful with what you decide to try and change about her. Change her habits, but not her nature.

The assistant principal at Foshay was adept at keeping her disappointment in perspective, and as a result, things started to get better for the ninth-grader in the inner city soon enough too. Her audition was a breakthrough and she was noticed at last. Under the wing of the assistant principal, her dependencies were recognized and dealt with, and her grades began to stabilize in the C-plus area, and after another audition she made it into the choir. She did not become a teenage mother either. While she still faces many challenges and difficulties, she is bright with hope and looking forward to a better future.

WRONG? BE
COMPLETELY WRONG

꩜

At some point when you are dealing with your adolescent daughter or son, you will get the whole thing completely ass-backward. You will mistrust her when she is very trustworthy. You will blame him when he is blameless. You will be suspicious of something very innocent. You will accuse when you should just shut the heck up. You will give a whole speech about the importance of good grades and then realize that you are looking at last year's report card. You will be unsure of exactly what time she said she was coming home and jump on her for being late even though she is actually on time. At some point, you will find yourself utterly in the wrong.

As you try to figure your way out of the mess you have made, consider the joy and absolute freedom that comes with being absolutely and completely wrong. No need to apologize with excuses and illogical explanations. No need to diminish her rightness while dismissing your wrongness.

No reason to explain that you are almost correct if things are just viewed from a slightly different angle. No purpose in demonstrating in great detail why you are not quite *as* incorrect as it may appear. Suck it up, recruit. Hold your mud. Marvel with her about how ridiculous you must have looked and agree with her on how boorish you were. Accept *complete* responsibility for your behavior. Defending a quarter-inch of dignity is pointless! Simply let it go. Gladly let it go.

Make your apologies to your daughter real and meaningful, no matter how small the infraction. Be completely sorry for whatever it is that you have done. Let it be totally your fault. If it is your fault that the family missed a flight or you made the dinner reservations for the wrong night, accept the blame completely and apologize just as completely. No need for caveats or explanations or anything that takes away from the wrong you have committed.

Maybe you did not think that retrieving your daughter from a party in front of all of her friends at eleven p.m. on the dot was a boorish maneuver, but *she* thought so. And that's the point. She was embarrassed and humiliated by what you did. You may have made the wrong decision, even if it was for all the right reasons. Even if you were a little bit right, you were still very, very wrong. Regardless of how incrementally correct you may have been, apologize to her for the overwhelmingly wrong part, mustering all the humility and sincerity that you possibly can.

If you follow this guideline, you will also give your daughter an incredible gift that she can use the rest of her life. You will show her *how to be wrong* and *how to be sorry when she is wrong*. You will show her how to admit to a mistake and how to apologize for it. You will provide her with a template that she can use in all of her relationships going forward.

The parents who defend their shattered decorum and tattered dignity with detailed arguments just make things much worse. When you have acted the boor, just admit it. When you are sorry, be very sorry. When you are wrong, be completely wrong.

LET THEM
BE BEAUTIFUL

Sheryl is a wonderful and giving woman. She owns her own business, is still in love with her husband after more than twenty years of marriage, volunteers all over the place, and is the kind of person who puts a smile on people's faces when they meet her. One of her roles in the community for many years was to serve as commissioner of the high school boys' basketball league. Not that she knows all that much about being a basketball commissioner—or about basketball, frankly. She once referred to a free throw as a "free thingy." But it was a job that needed to be done and so she did it. That's how we met.

One evening I found myself with several other coaches over at her house for that year's draft of players. Sheryl introduced us to her family. Nice husband, handsome son, and a daughter who was probably eleven or twelve at the time, with long blond hair flying everywhere. She was really striking—like Cybill Shepherd might have looked as a child. But not just beautiful on the outside: You could tell right away from the way she spoke with her mother and father that she was a thoughtful and loving daughter, i.e., beautiful on the inside too. If you were Walt Disney, you would say, "Okay, we just found Cinderella." If you were France, you might put her on a coin.

I saw Sheryl a few days later and complimented her on the successful draft, and on her home and family. Regarding her daughter, I said, as an aside, "Now, don't go cutting all her hair off for no good reason, okay?" I said it completely as a joke, not even really expecting a reply. But her response was very real and immediate. She said, "You mean like my mother did to me?"

There at the Coffee Bean, right by the sugar bar, Sheryl told me the story of herself and her mother, many years ago, when Sheryl was about the same age as her daughter was now. While they were visiting her grandmother's house, her mother tackled her one afternoon, held her down on the floor, and chopped off all of her beautiful long hair. Without explanation, without discussion, she just cut it off. Sheryl told the story in such detail that I was there with her. I heard the scissors, I heard shoes fly off and feet hit the floor in the scuffle, I heard an adolescent girl crying out, "Why are you doing this . . . ?" over and over. Sheryl still had so many regrets about that day. It was an unforgettable moment in her life. A scarring moment.

Sheryl told me that for a long time her mother never

explained why she had done what she had. Why would a mother ever deliberately make her daughter *less* beautiful? Why would a mother ever take away a daughter's emerging sense of self and self-respect? The questions kept getting asked but never getting answered. Until many years later, when Sheryl's mother finally admitted that maybe she was just a little bit envious of her daughter and how beautiful she was becoming.

Unfortunately, as I have come to learn, Sheryl is only one of many people who have had to deal with a forced physical transformation at the hands of their often well-meaning but somewhat misguided parents.

How many times have you seen a girl, say, ten, eleven, or twelve, who has always enjoyed her long and beautiful hair show up at school one day and it's all cut off. Tuesday it was trailing her like a comet's tail. Wednesday she looked like Mia Farrow in *Rosemary's Baby*. When the hair goes, with it often goes a big chunk of her personality, her individuality, her fingerprint in the universe, and sometimes her statement of self-purpose. For the next several weeks the daughter walks around looking like a freshly shorn sheep, stepping awkwardly, her balance different, her signature altered. There are learned researchers who know much more than I do about the long-term impact situations like this may have on a girl's life over time. But as a practical matter, I wish it would never happen at all.

Cutting off children's hair against their will is not only

not great parenting, it is incredibly insensitive. Surprise your adolescent or teenage child with something wonderful, not something tragic, and not by forcing a drastic and dramatic change in her aesthetics. Take her out to the movies, not down to the barbershop. Question your own motives before you make a radical change in her physical appearance. Is your motivation fashion or punishment? Are you following a trend or just being dominant? Will your child celebrate this day or remember it as one of the worst days of her life? Are you being practical or are you being unnecessarily precious? Most of the adolescent and teenage children I know do not like it at all when anything is forced on them, especially in respect to their physical appearance and the picture they present to the world.

But this is not just about hair. This is really about showing complete respect to the adolescent or teenage person in your life, allowing her to become who she is supposed to become. Whenever possible, let her decide her clothes, her sports, her fashions, her passions, and her hair. Let her make her own beauty statements. Force nothing on her other than your love and devotion. Have faith in her ability to ultimately make the right decision, and trust that she will. When there is not enough joy and happiness in the world, there is nothing at all wrong with letting your children be beautiful, in whatever way *they* want to be beautiful.

SOMETHING I LEARNED
ON THE *TODAY* SHOW

❋

I had the opportunity to sit with Mr. George Foreman and Mr. Matt Lauer as a guest on the *Today* show during the initial marketing campaign for *Parking Lot Rules*. The subject was fatherhood, and both George Foreman and I had written books on the subject. There was a third guest, another gentleman, Mr. Roland Warren, who was president of the National Fatherhood Initiative. He did not pronounce his name like it was spelled; instead of "Row-lund," he pronounced it "Raw-lund." When Mr. Lauer joined us on set, at practically the last second, he sat down, adjusted his mike, said hello to George and me, and then said hello to Mr. Warren and mispronounced his name. I looked around to see if anybody was going to say something, but nobody said anything. Who wants to correct Matt Lauer on his own show? By a remarkable and odd coincidence, my book had a rule *just* for a situation like this. It was Rule 31: Say the Awkward with a Question. It is a technique I developed to help parents save their children embarrassment when the children mispronounce a word or get a fact wrong or say someone's name incorrectly. The only problem was that I had never tried this rule out on an adult. Until then. The clock was counting down to the end of commercial. 11. 10. 9. I turned to Mr. Lauer and said, "If you were pronouncing his name incorrectly, would you want us to tell you?" He said, "Of course, yes, please . . ." and so we told him. "Raw-lund," not "Row-land." Mr. Lauer looked over at Roland and smiled and made a note on his card. He said, "Glad we found that out . . ." and then, next thing I know, we're on the air.*

In that informative little exchange I saw that the rules I had written to make life better for children and parents also worked very well for first-time authors selling books on morning television shows with legendary hosts. But then I learned something that I have never ever forgotten.

During the course of the interview, Mr. Roland ("Raw-lund") Warren brought up the point that children often use and mean and spell important life words differently from how adults do. He gave as an example the word "love." What it means to adults is practically indescribable. What it means to children is basically this: How much time are we spending together? And for that reason children spell the word "love" T-I-M-E. Hearing him say this opened a door for me. He made me realize that there are many words

*To see the *Today* show segment, go to www.parkinglotrules.com.

and phrases adolescents and teenagers use when they really mean to say something else, something very different. Or they will say nothing and expect us to understand what that means too. Or when they cannot find the exact words that they need to describe an uncomfortable feeling, they use completely different words that are more comfortable. I knew lots of these words and phrases, but until I heard Mr. Warren say that children spell "love" T-I-M-E, I did not know that I knew them.

Just in case there are any parents in the same situation, below are some alternative meanings and definitions of several key words and phrases that I have discovered in the adolescent and teenage lexicon. What they say is on the left, what I think they mean is on the right.

THE WORDS THEY SAY	THE WORDS THEY MEAN
Love.	Time.
Love me.	Spend more time with me.
Just listen, for once . . .	Please be more patient with me.
Go away, just leave me alone.	Find me, I might be lost.
You never show me that you love me.	You might not love me.
You don't understand.	You don't want to understand.
You are not being fair.	You are judging me without the evidence. . . .
Trust me.	Obviously you don't trust me.

THE WORDS THEY SAY	THE WORDS THEY MEAN
I don't care, at all.	I care, I care, I care. . . .
You're not listening to me.	You do not listen to me.
You must think I am deaf.	Why are you yelling at me?
Can I have $50?	I have no concept of the value of money.
Can I have a car?	I am too young to have a car.
I have no friends.	My friends are having fun without me.
Stay out of my room!	Please stay out of my room.
Do you like the way I look?	Please, just notice me.

One of our principal responsibilities as parents is to simply listen. Listen, listen, listen. If we try hard enough to listen to them, we might actually hear what our adolescents and teenagers are trying to tell us about themselves, their lives, their views, their dreams, and their reason for being here. It's not always what they say; often it is what they mean.

WHAT RIVERS TEACH
ABOUT ADOLESCENTS

I recently flew back to Los Angeles from New York and passed over several rivers along the way. I looked down in wonder and awe at the Mississippi, the Missouri, and the Colorado. Each one cut through the earth's skin almost indiscriminately, creating a mosaic of grooves and tricks and patterns. Rivers are one of nature's greatest gifts. Rivers can do so many things, they almost have intelligence. They can change constantly and are never the same from one second to the next. They can protect themselves from pollutants and fungus by pounding these enemies into submission on their shores and bottoms. They can grow and shrink. They provide regular harvests of fish and oxygen. They force thousands upon thousands of tons of water through pulsing tributaries and gorged gulleys, and in so doing, provide those of us here at the top of the food chain with all the power and light we need. Their origins can sometimes begin literally miles deep within the earth and travel for several more miles under the surface before the headwaters even begin. By any standard, rivers are amazing things.

But as much as it accomplishes and achieves every day of its extraordinary life, have you ever noticed how disorganized and all over the place an individual river is? At least from high above. The irregularities that mark its path? The back and forth, right and left, up and down? The mistakes and the corrections? A river never travels in a straight line. It meanders all over the place. It can change its course so frequently that it looks like the scrawling of a first-grader's first try at cursive writing. But this is natural, nature in action—mistake, correction, mistake, correction, mistake, correction. Looking down on the Colorado River's carving out of the Grand Canyon struck me as a testament to one river's ability to pursue and accomplish its destiny, without any help from anyone or anything. The Colorado did that all by itself, making and correcting millions of little mistakes along the way.

To me, the same knowledge gained from watching a great river can be applied directly to the raising of amazing adolescents and teenagers. Not every mistake needs to be corrected. Not every step needs a suggestion for a better step. Not every way requires a better way. Not every choice requires the parent to offer a cache of better choices. Not every situation needs helpful advice.

As often as you can bear it, let your adolescents and teenagers make their own decisions—even if you do not agree completely and even if those decisions appear to you to be incorrect. At the end of the day, the decisions or choices may not be so important that each one needs to be corrected. These little steps and little missteps may just be your daughter figuring out the path she is *supposed* to be taking. Possibly the "two steps forward, one step back" approach is keeping her from moving too far forward too fast. A few little zigzags here and there could be your son's way of tapping on the brakes, instinctively ensuring that he does *not* complete a part of his journey before he is ready to complete it. Mistake, correction, mistake, correction. Just like a river.

Parents, mentors, coaches, and teachers must ask themselves which is better, correcting mistakes or allowing them to correct themselves. Making suggestions about every tiny step or letting an adolescent figure out for herself which path is the best one for her. Encouraging her to rely on your instinct or encouraging her to begin to trust her own. Allowing an adolescent to choose her own path and find that she does not like it after all, or choosing for her and leaving her to wonder if that was one of the great mistakes of her life. Ultimately, we have to ask ourselves this question: What good will it do to teach an adolescent or teenager to override her instinct and be deaf to her own natural warning system?

But at the same time, at what point exactly should adolescents be allowed to start making their own decisions, and thus begin to learn to live with the consequences of their own decisions?

I am in the middle of one of these dilemmas right now. As I write this, my son Sam is twelve, about to turn seventeen. He is his own boy in most every way, knows what he likes and does not like, knows himself already very well. Sam has grown tired of one of my favorites of his sports. I did not even know soccer existed when I was his age, so to see him out there is a kind of rebirth. There is something consuming and beautiful about watching him compete, a servant to the game, his face alive with passion, sweaty, with mud or grass stains on his brightly colored uniform. I love the sharp contrast of the green grass against the shocking white of the big numbers on his back—it was 24 this last year. I watch him play, and the sight of the tremendous effort he puts forth to defend, steal, pass, or block a shot or score a goal somehow justifies my belief in him, and encourages and enhances my devotion to him. It fulfills me to see him attempt greatness, even if it is just in an American Youth Soccer Organization boys' U12 soccer game. Maybe it does more for me than it does for him. But from a spot on the sidelines of the really big games, tournaments, and the like, I watch him stand in the middle of the field, with his hands on his hips, catching his breath, while the small crowd of parents shouts out, "Nice play, Sam . . . Good work out there . . . Way to play, Sam . . ." and it makes my heart nearly burst with pride that my boy is doing such things. Things I never did.

But now he wants to stop. He's had enough. He wants to hang up his worn-down cleats and smelly shin guards for the last time. He's had plenty of the five a.m. wake-ups and two-hour drives. He's tired of tournaments where his team waits all afternoon to play in a game and then gets shellacked. He is done with two long practices each week and the criticisms of his coach in a clipped and stern British accent. He's grown much less fond of losing, even to amazing teams. But he's not just good at soccer, he's great at soccer. He is the starting sweeper on a great club team. He can put the ball in the net from the half line, if necessary. He is a force on the field. He shuts down almost every attack that is directed at him and rarely loses hope or heart, regardless of the likelihood of the outcome. He encourages his teammates and helps up the boys that he knocks down. The very best of him shows up when he is in a soccer match.

But he believes that he has reached the end. He wants to grow up and begin to make his own decisions. He thinks that he has outgrown soccer. Meanwhile, for some reason I cannot explain, my heart aches. Is it the right or wrong thing to do, to allow my child to stop a sport he is great at but may no longer have a love for? Is it a big mistake he is making? Or am I the one making the big mistake?

I ask myself: Should I let him make his own decision?

Should I let him choose to do what he wants to do, or choose for him? Should I let him take this amazing game out of his life, just because he wants to? Should I let him make a decision he may regret, or have him delay that decision for a year or two? Let him make a mistake—and thus learn from it—or make the decision for him and let him wonder what might have been? Force him to play a sport because I still love it, or let him quit a sport because he has tired of it? He said to me recently, "Just because I'm good at something doesn't mean I have to do it."

I spoke with his mom, and his brother, and other dads, and finally found my answer. More important than how I feel about it, I want him to be in touch with his own instincts. I want him to hear the voice of his own truth. I want him to know the feel of his own decision-making process. I want him to begin to be responsible for the choices that he makes and to realize that his choices will affect his whole life, not just next soccer season. Maybe he will make a better decision later in his life because he gets to make this decision today.

That's what I learned from watching those rivers. Adolescents and teenagers have to learn to make their own choices, live with their own decisions, be responsible for their own behavior, and correct their own mistakes.

someday may already be here

❋

Thomas will soon be at the end of his teenage years; as I write this, he is eighteen going on thirty. He shaves and has his own taste in music, clothes, style, and life. He has his own opinions and points of view and is not the least bit shy about sharing them, either one-on-one at the Starbucks, or on his daily blog to thousands of people. It was a very long time ago when I promised a newborn boy sleeping in my arms that I was going to be the greatest daddy ever. The years have gone by in the blink of an eye, but oh, what a beautiful blink . . . A million throws and catches and kicks, hundreds of films we saw and shared, thousands of miles traveled to school and work and soccer and once to Paris, and an unending memory of conversations and ideas shared. Truthfully, possibly twenty bad days altogether.

Of course, now lost in the mists of his memories are the crises of bad grades and lackluster efforts, time wasted, punishments enforced, and those few regrettable moments lost to anger and frustration with his behaviors and his poor time management. But at this point, I do not think he could care less about any or all of that. All he knows is that he made it . . . this far, anyway. He graduated from high school with only a couple of bumps and bruises along the way. His adolescent and teenage years did not ruin him or take away his spirit, and they did not leave him without a dream. He is a great guy, already. He is busy discovering who he is supposed to be, and he is becoming the very best version of that person imaginable. If the first big part of life was a test that he was given, he is through and he passed with flying colors. He has a job, a high school diploma, a big dream, a girlfriend, some money in his pocket. He is on his way. He is in the game.

It never occurred to me that his adolescence and teenage years would be the adventure they turned out to be, back when I knew nothing, back when it started, back when he was just a cute eleven-year-old. I never thought I would really care all that much about a high school diploma until I saw him walk up there and pick one up. He said he could hear me sighing with relief from the stage, and I was the width of a football field away—in the bleachers. Looking back on our first two decades together, the highs were really much higher than I imagined and the lows were not really all that bad, at least now that I am looking at them in perfect retrospect. I cannot say with certainty that I have always been the most graceful parent, or that I always said the right thing at the right time, or that I did exactly what was expected of me every single time it was expected of me. I know I overreacted in some circumstances and lost my head in others. I recall once parking down the street from a party Thomas had gone to at his friend Jake's house, just waiting for something to go wrong, and then driving off quite ashamed with myself for not trusting in him. If I made mistakes, which I am sure I did, they were honest and careful ones, and most were on the side of too much parenting, never not enough.

He asked me something a few weeks ago that literally left me breathless, it was so revealing. He said, "Do you wish I had been someone else? Do you wish I had been a different boy?" I could hardly even respond. Finally I said, "Do I wish you had gotten better grades? Yes. Do I wish you had been offered a full ride at Harvard playing golf or lacrosse? Yes. Do I wish you had taken better advantage of the many incredible opportunities I threw down before you? Absolutely yes. But do I wish you were another boy, someone else, different in any way? Never. Absolutely never. The thought never once crossed my mind. If I ever said or did anything that made you think I felt that way, I take it back and will deny having ever said it. You are perfect just the way you are, kid."

But boy, oh boy, what this question reveals . . . It says that after all the time and effort, kindness and love, devotion and disappointment, punishments, tutors, trips, advice, emergency rooms, PTA meetings, coaching, practices, play-offs, counseling, and on and on and all the rest, he still does not realize just how much I did it all just *for* him, just so he could *be* him, just so he could have *his* life. That I adore him, completely, and with all of me, forever, just exactly the man he is turning out to be.

My mom used to say that you can never really repay your parents for what they do for you. The only way to balance the scales is to give your children the best of what you have to offer them, and never count your good deeds. I did not understand this for a long time but I understand it now. I can say without any doubt in my heart that I have given my Thomas everything I had to offer as a father, and that I tried every day to be the very best father that I could be. I gave him my everything and my all. Gladly.

The adventure is just now starting all over again with Sam, who is just now twelve. Sam watched his brother make plenty of mistakes and get in too much trouble too many times and hopefully realizes that he does not have to make those same mistakes and get in that same trouble. I am sure that he will make entirely different mistakes and get into completely different kinds of trouble. But that is another book for another day. Sam is an extraordinary person. Gifted and funny, polite and respectful, and totally comfortable around all the adults he meets. As his adolescent and teenage years await, I am watching with trepidation and excitement these last few days of his childhood ebb away.

Only once in a great while now, when it's just the two of us off somewhere, I will hear him speak like a little boy and say softly, "Da-da . . . my Da-da . . ." to which I respond, "Sam and the Daddy-boy . . . Off on another whirlwind adventure!!" Just like we have been saying since he was two and we heard that line in one of the Shrek films, long before adolescence was even a thought. I am enjoying every single moment of every day I get with him and I treasure the final few precious seconds of his childhood as they race by me. At the same time, I can hardly wait to meet the man who is soon to be revealed.

THE SHAQUILLE O'NEAL RULE: BE NICE EVERY CHANCE YOU GET

꩜

I worked for Shaquille O'Neal many years ago, running his record company TWISM Records. This stands for The World Is Mine, a phrase you can see tattooed on his arm. I signed him to his first songwriting/music publishing deal when he was an NBA rookie, just out of Louisiana State University, and he returned the favor by hiring me when I found myself, as we say, between situations.

Success in the music business is all about brand building and relationships, asking for and giving favors, making the most of opportunities wherever they may arise, and being ready and willing to do what it takes, when it takes, how it takes, to make sure the world hears your new music. We were promoting one of the best of his five albums, *You Can't Stop the Reign*, and looking for cross-promotions when a situation presented itself. The hospital where Shaquille was born had asked him for some money to fund a prenatal care unit and he had obliged them with a large check. Shaq and his entourage—which included former New Jersey police-men Uncle Mike and Uncle Jerome, and former trouble-makers Cousin Kenny and Cousin Dirt—and I traveled to New Jersey to dedicate the wing of the hospital and honor the doctor who had delivered him, and possibly pick up a few headlines and mentions for the new album as part of the adventure.

So on a Saturday morning, a crowd of us were driving in two oversized SUVs down a wide empty street in Newark toward the hospital; there was not a soul to be seen, either walking or in a car, anywhere in our view, in any direction, except for one individual. About a quarter mile up ahead was a boy bouncing a basketball, daydreaming his way through his morning, and by some unreal coincidence he was wearing a very bright and very gold, very oversized, very noticeable Shaquille O'Neal Lakers jersey. You could see the big 34 on his back from all the way across town. He stood out like a sunflower in a parking lot. Talk about chance and circumstance . . . This was a wow moment just waiting to happen.

Shaquille loves children of all ages and is always looking for ways to be kind and generous and influential, and this opportunity was no different from a slam dunk alley-oop to win a big game. He told the driver to pull the cars up right next to the boy and told everyone else to just sit tight, to do nothing. We just sat there for maybe ten or fifteen sec-onds, motors rumbling, waiting. Up close the kid looked to be about twelve or thirteen, just at the beginning of his adolescence. African-American, and a little scared, though not so scared that he was running off. His sense of curiosity was piqued, clearly, and whose wouldn't be? He had no idea what these two cars were doing just sitting there right next to him. We could have been wise guys, movie stars, frankly anybody. He didn't know who was inside, or what he had done to deserve the attention. Shaquille slowly rolled down his window, and their eyes met. As the lowering glass finally revealed to the boy whom he was looking at, the expression on his face grew into one of such wonder and disbelief it was something I had never seen. It was like a cartoon, the way his face changed. Once he was sure it was Shaquille, the boy blinked a couple of times, swallowed hard, thought of something to say and then thought better of it, licked his lips, looked around, jittered and laughed, and then didn't know what to do. He was actually just a couple of feet away from one of his neighborhood's greatest success stories, one of the NBA's greatest superstars, and, from what I could see, his favorite player and idol. He could hardly even exhale he was so breathless. Shaquille smiled at him, handed him a $100 bill, and simply said, "Shhhhh . . ." With his other hand he gestured to the driver to start moving. Our cars glided back into the street, and we resumed our trip to the hospital, only a minute or two behind schedule. I looked back out the rear window to see how the boy was taking it, and what I saw was so beautiful it was permanent. Once seen, never unseen. I kind of knew and kind of hoped what I might see, but this picture was even better. He looked like he was an acrobat, jumping in the air, letting out shrieks and whoops I could not hear, hardly able to contain himself. He was literally jumping with joy. It was hilarious and touching and unreal and forever. It put an image like a snapshot in my mind that I will never let go of.

I will never forget the boy, or the day, or Shaquille's unexpected kindness. There were no cameras, no one recording the event, no discussion of posterity or blogs or tweets; it was an act he chose to do for no other reason than to be nice. Shaquille stopped and blew some magic dust into the life of an inner-city child who just happened to be walking down the street bouncing a basketball, wearing his jersey.

Shaquille could have done nothing, but that's not him. He could have noticed and had a laugh and looked the other way, but that's not him either. He could have told our driver to just keep driving, but he is unable, I think, to resist his instinct and the chance to be nice to someone, especially a child.

It was such a simple act of kindness, and such a cool thing to do, so easy, and it brought so much joy. Ever since, I have looked for opportunities to do nice things for my sons Thomas and Sam, as well as the many other adolescents and teenagers in my life. Sometimes it may be as simple as a smile and a hello. Or I may reach out to offer a quick trip to the nearest Baskin-Robbins, even when a punishment is being enforced. Or we might play a little basketball in the middle of preparations for the SATs, which we slept through the first two times.

Yes, it is easier sometimes to walk by an adolescent or teenager and ignore an opportunity to be nice or to be kind. Maybe you are upset about something that was said or punishing her because of something that was done. Maybe there were some bad grades, or chores left uncompleted. So often it is too easy to say, "Well, I'll be nice later, right now I've got to teach this kid a lesson," and so forth. But suppose you took advantage of every chance to be nice to your adolescent or teenager, threw around an extra "Good Morning" or two, or blew her an extra good-night kiss. Suppose you found a few minutes to catch up on the details of a day, instead of rushing off somewhere. Suppose the dwindling slivers of sunlight at the end of a long afternoon of studying provide just enough light to throw a ball or take a quick walk around the neighborhood. A great conversation might appear out of nowhere and might be the only time that particular and unique conversation could ever take place. Your being generous may be the difference between a good day and a bad one. Your being loving may be the extra percentage of joy that swings an evening from lost to found. Your being kind is possibly the best of you, and the smile on your face may be the sign she has been hoping to see all evening. Your understanding may be the tiny event that changes everything about your adolescent or teenager's universe, at least that part of it.

Maybe you will never be one of the greatest NBA players in history. Maybe you will never get to wear four championship rings. Maybe you will never know what it is like to be Rookie of the Year, or Most Valuable Player in the finals, or the reason why your city is celebrating, again and again. But there is something you can do that is exactly like Shaquille O'Neal . . . Be nice every chance you get.

compliments

When Thomas was still very young and his adolescence was light-years away, I paid him too great a compliment one afternoon, and in so doing almost discouraged him from ever doing that particular thing ever again. We had been somewhere in town and saw someone's dad who we had not seen in at least a year. Out of nowhere, Thomas remembered the man's name and addressed him by it. I am terrible with names and this made such an impact on me because it saved me the embarrassment of asking the man who he was and how exactly I knew him.

When we got home, I was very complimentary to Thomas. I remarked, at least a couple of times, how amazed I was that he had been able to remember that man's name. But instead of smiling and reacting with pleasure to what I was saying, he slowly and deliberately brought his hands up to the sides of his head and covered his ears. Right in the middle of my big compliment! I asked him if something was wrong and he nodded as if to say yes. I asked Thomas whether he wanted me to stop complimenting him and he nodded yes again. Of course I stopped, and the conversation ended immediately, but I could not figure out what had happened and why.

I reached out to several people wiser than myself on the subject and no one gave me an answer that resulted in the epiphany I was looking for, until I asked my mom if she had any ideas. To her it seemed very simple. Thomas was covering his ears because he was not sure how he had done the thing that I was complimenting him for. After all, it was an intellectual accomplishment, not a physical one. Had he thrown a ball perfectly, he would know what he had done and would try to repeat it. Had he rolled in a nice long putt, that too would be something that he could repeat. But not so with his intellect. He did not know how he had done it, so he did not know how he could repeat it, and thus the compliment was more of a dare and a challenge than it was a recognition or a reward.

Ever since that day I have been so very careful of the kind, nature, and number of compliments that I pay to Thomas and all of the young people in my life. I never pass up an opportunity to pay a compliment, but I try to sprinkle my compliments in the air like little white birds of goodwill that will fly around long after the young people's acts have been forgotten and the compliments have disappeared. Never excessive anymore, and I deliver them now very specifically.

Compliments for brainpower (such as Thomas's remembering the man's name) are even more brief and to the point, almost like statements of fact.

Sam and I were driving back from golf. The newly remixed and remastered Beatles albums had just been released and we were listening from top to bottom to every single one. I was using the opportunity to give him a thorough and lasting introduction to this group of the greatest songwriters ever. As we started the fourth album, Sam said, "All the Beatles' songs are about love." He was twelve and he had already figured it out. I almost stopped the car to look over at him. It was unbelievable how his comment was so perfect and so accurate. How could he get that so exactly and precisely correct? I wanted to make a really big deal about his insight, and his intuition, and his intellect, and his innate ability to understand how some of the biggest pieces fit together when it comes to my favorite thing in the world, music.

I love the Beatles. Their songs are, to me, the greatest collection of pop songs ever created. I love their music even more now than I did when it was created, if that is even possible. Their songs are like old and dear friends now. So this moment with Sam was not just a moment, it was an incredible moment. I could have talked for many hours about how much it meant to me that he understood what the Beatles meant to the world. I could have gone on and on about Sam's intuitive ability, his understanding of music and lyrics, his innate wisdom, and how happy I was that he had gotten something so very complicated so very right.

But I remembered what had happened with Thomas many years before. I carefully considered the compliment I was going to give Sam before I gave it. I remembered all too well that a child does not need to be complimented excessively every time he does something amazing. I looked over at him and just said, "Brilliant, son. You got it exactly right." Nothing more. A smile spread across his face and his hands were nowhere near his ears.

PART THREE

BIG DREAMS

D reams are to childhood what blood is to life: vital, necessary, enriching. They pulse through the heads and hearts of our adolescent and teenage children every minute of every day. Dreams provide them with a vision of what's possible—they're like a hand reaching out for tomorrow. Dreams provide your son or daughter with more than just a direction in life—dreams can provide that life.

Many wise people have said many wise things about the importance of dreams in a life, and by inference in the life of an adolescent or teenager, including Henry David Thoreau ("Go confidentally in the direction of your dreams"), Aristotle ("Hope is a waking dream"), and Oprah ("The biggest adventure . . . is to live the life you dream").

I could not agree more with these dreamers. Following are some ideas on dreams, both big and small, what they do and what they can do, what they mean and what they can mean, and what value they can bring to a life.

sometimes a big dream is all you have

꧁ ꧂

There was a moment in my life when all I had left was a dream. I was fourteen years old, living at the Synanon Ranch, separated from my family, the home lost. It was just dawning on me what a terrible mistake this whole thing had been. I was like Pinocchio at the part in the story where he starts to become a donkey. I had been very happy to tend to the horses instead of to math, to learn belt weaving instead of economics, to show big donors around the property instead of learning to write compelling papers. I left all matters of education lost and forgotten by the wayside. But by not attending school, I was way off track and falling behind my peers in the education races, with no way to know just how far away the finish line was.

This is one of the biggest problems with adolescence. You have no idea how bad things are going until it's practically too late to do anything about it.

As I was beginning to realize just how big a hole I had

dug for myself, I started thinking of how I was going to get out of this particular hole. They were parallel emerging thoughts. The only thing I could control completely was my dreams—nobody could take those away. So I dreamed myself the biggest dream I could imagine. It was imperfect, imprecise, and illogical, but it was a big beautiful dream. I was going to become . . . a veterinarian! A large-animal vet no less, looking after cows and horses and all of the other large animals that I was taking care of instead of studying algebra and chemistry and other subjects I would need to actually become a veterinarian. But I attached myself to this dream like a barnacle to the side of a tramp steamer. I read every single book that James Herriot, the great British veterinarian and author, wrote, and I would imagine the thrill of delivering lambs in the middle of rainstorms and rescuing lost horses from swollen rivers. For years I fell asleep watching myself single-handedly saving a herd of cattle or carefully withdrawing molars from unhappy sheep in my mobile hospital. I even found a book on equine diseases and started memorizing the hundreds of ways that a horse can perish. I told anyone who would listen about my big dream and how I was going to accomplish it. After a while, I even started to believe it was going to happen. Becoming a veterinarian was the one thing that I had with me every day and every night, the one thing I had that would never let me down, the one thing that I was completely sure of. While it was true that I did not have much, I had a glimmering hope that lived with me every single moment of every single day. I had a big dream.

Many teenagers and adolescents find it difficult to see any part of their future. It is a crowded and difficult picture to look at, much less to try to understand. Often adolescents do not know that they can even have a big dream, or they consider it childish and immature to be imagining their future at all. But a big dream can cut through the clutter and make things clear that previously were murky. A big dream can bring perspective and hope to an otherwise unaccomplished or faltering child. A big dream can transport an adolescent from a challenging situation to a winning one, with ease and grace.

Parents must be careful, gentle, and respectful when helping an adolescent or teenager identify her big dream. Encouraging her to let down her guard long enough to look and see what is actually behind it there in the dreamy darkness will take a lot of careful, thoughtful effort. Try not to destroy the habitat while searching for the butterfly. When she finally divulges what her big dream is—be filled with wonder. Say nothing logical or practical. Try not to be wise. No head scratching or wrinkled noses or long, deep sighs that would damn her newborn dream before it even walks. No doubting a big dream before it has a chance to fly.

Sometimes a big dream is all you have.

A BIG DREAM IS JUST TRANSPORTATION

A new big dream is like a brand-new car. Shiny and new, clean as a whistle, never gone a mile, never been scratched or dented, never been anything, and it even has that new-dream smell. This is the "vehicle" that your son will be driving around in for the next few years, hopefully keeping it spotless, and always showing it to his friends. He will be driving it right into his future.

Maybe in his dream he is a doctor, a baseball player, or a musician, or owns his own modeling agency or runs a charity, or is doing something else that touches his passion and scratches at the windshield of his tomorrow. Just like a real car, it does not really matter which brand or make or style it is. All that matters is that he has something to get around in.

A big dream is a peek at an imagined future, a glimpse of a possible life. It is one prism through which to view the rest of what his life might become. It should be imagined down to the very last detail, as much and as often as possible. The adolescent or teenage driver never knows when the dream will stop working for him, when and if it will be taken from him, or when it will crash and burn and be left on the side of a road somewhere. The important thing is to have a very specific and realizable dream, full of possibility and hope. What is a big dream if not a way to look ahead?

When I was about fourteen, more than anything else in the world, I wanted to be a veterinarian. There was one very big problem. I also discovered right around that same time that I was incredibly and terribly allergic to any animal that had fur or feathers. This is to say almost every animal except for a particularly rare breed of cat known as the Canadian Hairless. I would see a picture of a goat and sneeze. I would imagine a dog scratching behind his ear and get that tickly feeling in my throat. A barn swallow would start to warble and my eyes would start to water.

There was another big problem that I discovered a few years later. There were a lot of people who had the same big dream as me, and most of them also ended up in the pre-veterinary program at the University of California–Davis, home of the best vet school in the world, and the college I miraculously got into. Unfortunately, I simply did not have the in-depth understanding of algebra or chemistry required to go along with my big beautiful dream. These were just two of the fundamental courses that one must zoom through with flying colors in order to make it into a veterinary school. Little did I know, but I was finished before I even began. I had the intellectual equivalent of a car up on cinder blocks with no motor. I was getting D's and F's in all my pre-vet courses, while all of the future veterinarians were getting A-pluses and invitations to the professor's house on weekends to sample his spicy shrimp gumbo. Not me. My test scores were dreadful, my notes looked like ancient Gaelic texts, and my lab sessions often ended quite suddenly—with shattered petri dishes, broken glass beakers, and someone calling the maintenance department to please refill the fire extinguisher. Again.

But I kept trying my hardest, my absolute hardest, every single day. That's how much I loved my big dream, and that was all I knew how to do anyway. If they were going to take it away from me, it was going to be a battle to the end. So I hired a tutor. I stayed up until all hours memorizing atom behavior and the periodic table of the elements. I dated a chemistry major. All for nothing, as it turned out. The whole thing came to a sudden end near the end of spring quarter when the UC–Davis chemistry department blithely informed me *in writing* that I had achieved the lowest grade in the department's history and that I no longer needed to attend classes. Had I not tried at all and just thrown darts at a board, I probably would have done at least as well. The letter was the end of the road for that particular dream. It was like watching smoke pour from under the hood of my beautiful car. I pulled over but all I could do was watch it go up in flames. There was no chance. It was finished. That dream was over.

So, just like that, I left behind what I had treasured all those years, and got on with finding a new dream. Even though I was studying at a world-renowned agricultural college, the last thing I had any interest in at that point was anything remotely agricultural. Grapes the size of peaches? Featherless chickens? Bimolecular cattle that could not stand up because they literally had too much meat on their bones? No, thanks. I moved to the next item on my list of loves: music. I looked through the UC–Davis handbook of possible degrees and found that a lovely little degree in music was available and that, coincidentally, it had no chemistry requirement. "Music major" had a nice ring to it, so I filled out all the papers and made the change and have never looked back or regretted the choice even one day since. I had a brand-new dream to drive around in. It was shiny and new. Clean as a whistle. Never gone a mile. Never been scratched or dented. Never been anywhere, and yes, it even had that new-dream smell.

A successful life requires flexibility. It also requires one to have the ability to tell when a big dream has come to the end of its possibilities. A lot of them do. A big dream just gets your teenager from one point in his life to another—

GROW THE TREE YOU GOT

maybe from ten to fourteen, or maybe twelve to eighteen. Or maybe your child will be a lucky one and will drive the same big dream throughout his life. The big dream is a vehicle that will keep him moving forward during his moments of greatest challenges, difficult choices, triumphs, and/or embarrassments. Yes, of course there will be many other factors and forces that will come to bear upon his adolescence and teenage life as well, but he will have his big dream to guide him through them.

The effect on me of having had such perfectly clear big dreams was the gift of purpose. Because of those big dreams I began to think that I had a reason for being here. I had something that I was supposed to do, something bigger than the present day. I had a future, and a beautiful way to get there.

I have never gotten out of the habit of having big dreams and drive several of them to this day. I still dream of being one of the greatest dads ever, becoming one of the greatest music publishers ever, and always being a better teacher, mentor, and volunteer. All the while I dream of being a great husband to my new wife and a great friend to my ex-wife. I dream big of being a generous and respectful man in all that I do. These are several of my biggest dreams. They move me from place to place, from day to day, from heartache to triumph. They get me wherever I need to go.

A big dream is just transportation.

embrace her
biggest dream

I was visiting recently with some students at the James A. Foshay Learning Center, an inner-city Los Angeles public school that is in the heart of Gangville, where innocence is at a premium, where students have a "street face" they have to wear whenever walking from home to school, and where most know someone who is incarcerated. I have made regular visits to this school for thirteen years. It is part of my volunteerism. After making sure that they all shook my hand like young ladies and gentlemen and looked me in the eye while doing so, I asked them, "What is your biggest dream today?" You would not think this would be a difficult question to answer, but for one girl, surprisingly, it was.

Her name was Brenda. She had no biggest dream, she had no big dream, she had no sense of what purpose would be served by having one anyway. She had no way of understanding the prescient value that dreams could bring to her life. She was fourteen and in eighth grade. To judge from the makeup and clothes, she looked like she was almost twenty and ready to audition for a part in a Sylvester Stallone movie about girls growing up too fast. She told me that nobody had ever asked her about her dreams before. She then told me and the whole group of students a little more about her chaotic and hectic household, and I understood why there was never time for anyone to really talk about ephemeral things like big dreams.

In her journey thus far, many of her littlest dreams had been overwhelmed and drowned out in the noise of a loud house and a very loud dad. He was a big guy with a big voice, and plenty to say. Her little dreams were being subsumed in the endless details of a big family living its many lives. I do not think it was intentional, but by not embracing her dreams, her parents were teaching her how *not* to dream. By not encouraging her dreams, her parents were showing her how *not* to reach for all the possibilities life might have to offer. By not helping her build her own dream, her parents were handcuffing her to theirs. By not pushing her to commit to a big dream, they were not encouraging her to even dream at all. She was being pushed not to try her hardest at living her life. With no big dreams to point her in the right direction, she was being held down, and she was holding herself back.

Turns out that Brenda is an extraordinarily creative person, particularly with lyrics and melodies. She cannot play an instrument, at least not yet, but she can write her own words and sing them with compelling passion. I hope she will sing on *American Idol* someday. She is alive whenever music is flowing through her, and it shows that this is possibly what she should be doing. I suggested that as a possible big dream she should create lyrics and melodies for other artists, or even for herself to perform. Maybe write songs for films and television shows, or even jingles for commercials. The big dream would be to write words and music, and wherever that path took her, it would take her. She never even knew that songwriting was an option! But once she began to consider it, it started to make more and more sense. Over the course of the next several visits, as her dream began to emerge and find its shape and form, I waited patiently for her to bring it up again, and show all of us what it was and how it would work in her life. Finally one day she did. She announced to the class that her biggest dream was to be a singer-songwriter. We all cheered.

Amid the challenges of her life in the inner city, with gangs and other negative influences shadowing her every day, in a Los Angeles public school, Brenda found a beautiful big dream. Like finding a rose growing in an asphalt yard. It was a beautiful and electrifying moment—watching someone lock in on her dream. I held her up to the other students as an example of what they could do too. We nurtured her dream before it was even an hour old and embraced it like a newborn puppy. I hope she reaches it, and just as much, I hope she will enjoy the journey with that beautiful dream clutched tightly in her hand.

Regardless of what you might expect or hope that your daughter's life turns out to be, the bridge to her future is really *her* dream for herself, not *your* dream for her. The path to the rest of her life is *her* hope for her future, not *your* wishes for everything to turn out just right. The meaning of life in *her* life will be her desire to fulfill her life's promises, not satisfying yours.

Let your daughter learn to look for the farthest star she can spot in the darkest of night skies, and name it after herself, name it after her biggest dream. Let her dream every day about that biggest dream, and whatever it is, you must find a way to embrace it and support its place in her life. You can dream anything you like for her to do or be, but it has no bearing whatsoever on what her life's dream is. You can suggest, but you cannot dream for her.

To see a very distant possibility, and then begin to dream about its likelihood and how it could fit into her life, is the beginning of your daughter's great adventure. Like Brenda, who dreams every night and day that she will one day be a songwriter.

Once identified, and once it appears, her biggest dream

should be embraced in all of its beauty and awkwardness, its newness to your child. Parents should welcome the big dream and all of its intricacies, especially just at its beginnings. When your daughter gathers her courage and brings you a newly discovered beautiful big dream, welcome it, be tender with it, love it, and enjoy it with her. Ask real and meaningful questions about it, and give her real and encouraging answers when she asks, "Do you really think I can . . . ?" In so doing, you will allow her to consider the possibility of the impossible.

BIG DReam,
LITTLe DReam

❀

One has to ask oneself: Why have a little dream. If you accomplish it, so what? What have you really accomplished? What do you do next? Have another little dream? In his book *Finishing the Hat*, Steven Sondheim quotes Leonard Bernstein as saying, "There is no point falling off the lowest rung of the ladder. If we are going to take a risk, let's take a huge risk." That comment inspired this:

LITTLE DREAM: Attend community college and become a nurse's aid.
BIG DREAM: Attend Harvard or Stanford for undergrad, then get into medical school at either, and become a world-renowned doctor who finds a cure for both cancer and wrinkles.

LITTLE DREAM: Go to New York and stay at the Plaza Hotel.

BIG DREAM: Go to New York and *buy* the Plaza Hotel. Rebuild it, re-pipe it, turn the dowdy old rooms into amazing apartments, and sell them for millions of dollars.

LITTLE DREAM: Work in the music business.
BIG DREAM: Spend a lifetime working in the music business, sign some of the greatest writers in the world, and sell 150 million singles and 250 million albums.

LITTLE DREAM: Become a community organizer.
BIG DREAM: Become an inspirational figure to millions of people all over the world, challenge the norm, break through every barrier, do things that have never been done before, get elected president.

Encourage your adolescent or teenager to dream his biggest dream, and who knows, he just might accomplish it.

SPOTTING a BIG DReam

I believe with all my heart that it is vitally important for teenagers to have a big dream that points them to their future. Not only to have a big dream, but to nurture it, garden it, believe in it, and keep it close by as part of their everyday imaginings and ruminations. But so often our teenagers and adolescents are intimidated by the fact of the future and what it might mean in their lives, and look at a big dream as one would look at a pair of handcuffs, as if a big dream were just another trap.

During conversations with many students about their future and how to get to it, I found that some lines of questions worked better than others in helping these young men and women discover what their big dream could be. I offer these questions as tools to help you and your teenager spot a big dream that would suit the type of life he wants and would be willing to sacrifice everything for. Or spot it and realize that that particular big dream is not worth the sacrifice, and that it is time to find another.

1. THE BIGGEST POSSIBLE DREAM? Let your teenager's big dream be a *really* big dream. There is no point in going to all the trouble of excavating and discovering a dream if it is in fact not that big after all. Encourage your teenager to make her big dream enormous, dynamic, earth-shattering, and possibly one that will change the world somehow. Here are some good starting points: Nobel Prize–winning scientist, Oscar-winning filmmaker, Grammy-winning musician or songwriter, Olympic gold medal sprinter. Ask your teen more than enough big questions and encourage her to aim as high as she can with her answers, and who knows, she just may decide she wants to be the first woman president, and wouldn't that be amazing!

2. WHAT WOULD HE DO FOR FUN? Now take money out of the equation, and for the sake of the exercise assume there that will be enough money. What would he do then, if money was not an issue? If the future was purely a matter of doing what he wanted to do, instead of doing what you wanted him to do, what would his big dream be? What would his

life be like if the future was all about "Why not?" instead of "Why?" If it was an option to do nothing, what would he dream of doing?

3. **WHAT WOULD BE A PERFECT DAY?** As an exercise, propose that your teenager imagine that all her biggest dreams came true. Encourage her to entertain the possibility that everything will go exactly right in her life. Possibly this includes going to a great high school and college; having a sterling athletic career at both, and amazing grades; graduating with an extra sash or two; and then enjoying life in a city of her choosing, anywhere in the world, doing precisely what she wants to do, with a love who adores her, whose father invented something very valuable, like Google, or Microsoft, or lithium batteries. Let her imagine a life where everything turned out to be exactly right . . . then what? What does she imagine her life would be like then? What would she do every day if every one of her little and big dreams came true?

4. **WHAT IS SHE PARTICULARLY GREAT AT?** Look at your daughter's life today without judgment or preconditions, more as a reporter writing a story. What does she like to do most? What are her favorite things to do with her time? What happens to all of her extra uncommitted minutes? Even if you do not

like the answers all that much, using the facts as they exist, help her discover what job or career she could have that would allow her to do that very thing every day as a career and a life. Whatever it is. Suppose that there is a career path right there, right under her nose. For instance, suppose that she is always on the phone with friends, discussing their problems and coming up with ideas and suggestions for how to make their lives better. Big dream? Doctor, psychologist, author, therapist, or teacher. Suppose that she is the one everyone borrows clothes and fashion ideas from before school starts or when a party is about to begin. Big dream? Couture, design, fashion consultant, talk show host, or magazine editor, and then let her see the director's cut of *The Devil Wears Prada*. Suppose that she always argues every point that you try to make and even has suggestions on how you could make those same points better. Big dream? Lawyer, writer, journalist, judge, or first female president. Suppose that she is a bit of a gossip and loves to tell you the stories of her day and how everyone at school interacted with everyone else at school. Big dream? News reporter, author, filmmaker, storyteller. You can see where this is going, right? Start the discussion without judgment, without it being another task, without her dreading the next part because it sounds like homework. Bring the conversation to her, make it feel like something interesting, and let it lead you closer to her big dream. Teenagers may not even realize that there is an opportunity to have a life doing exactly what it is that they would love to do most.

5. **WHAT HOBBY COULD BECOME HER CAREER?** Many adolescents discover a hobby, but they do not see it as having anything to do with their future, only as something that they love to do. Yet often a hobby can illuminate a path down which their future might walk, or it could actually be the path. Whether it is collecting, volunteering, writing, directing, making music, selling lemonade, cutting coupons, or running track. "If you can make your hobby your living, you'll never work a day in your life" is a saying in many cultures, including among the Irish. Ask your daughter about her hobbies, and see if there might be a career hiding in there somewhere, available to her simply by pursuing it for her living. You may spot her big dream hidden somewhere behind something she already loves to do.

6. **WHAT IS THE LIFESTYLE GOING TO BE?** Is money important? Does your teenager already have expensive habits and tastes? Does he care about the quality of life that would necessarily accompany his life? Or is he noncommittal about the way he wants

to live? His big dream should match the lifestyle to which he hopes to grow accustomed. If he needs fast cars and a nice penthouse apartment, then he should be dreaming about law school or medical school or about becoming an investment strategist or going into one of the other professions that pay big when you win big. If he couldn't care less how and where he lives, then a career as an actor or writer or teacher or music publisher is a completely reasonable big dream. Ask him how he wants to live.

The questions and discussions that I am encouraging will provide some answers and insights as to the big dreams and many possibilities that await your adolescent or teenager. She is just now beginning to imagine herself having a life other than the one she has with you. The design, imagining, and creation of a big dream is a step toward living in that new life. Her big dreams are forming but have not formed, so her answers and her ideas must be welcomed uninterrupted, allowed to reveal themselves, to evolve at her tempo.

It is important for a teenager to learn to please herself, not just her parents, when looking at her possible life or dreaming of her possible future. To see the world through her eyes. Let it be the acuity of her own vision that allows her to spot her big dream.

THE MAP TO THE
BIG DREAM

❦

The map is an exercise in discovery. It helps your child imagine the next ten years of her life—using a journey across America as a way of looking at her future. She will be taking a road trip from Los Angeles to New York, stopping in Santa Fe, Dallas, Chicago, and Atlanta along the way. Every leg of the journey is another two years of her life, and the whole trip will take ten years.

Each city represents a set of identifiable goals your daughter will have to meet in order to move successfully to the next city, step by step across the country, until she finally arrives at her destination, New York. The map, when completed, outlines the milestones your daughter will have to attain in order to live the life that she is dreaming of. It details how the next ten years will have to be spent to achieve her ultimate goals.

Your seventh-grader may be thinking she wants to go to medical school and specialize in pediatric dermatology.

Outline for her on the map how those next ten years will be spent, and she may decide that that is not the life she wants after all. (You can almost hear her saying, "Ten years of college . . . are you kidding me?") Or she may decide that it is *exactly* the life she wants. Either way, she is making the decision on what her life should be like, no one else. Your graduating senior may believe he has no future and really no big dreams at all, that it's all just an amorphous mess. But show him that he can go to college and law school before he gets out of Atlanta, and his view of his future could change dramatically.

The map is a tool that allows someone to telescope the future onto a piece of paper.

The map provides guidance for two principal vectors, time and accomplishment. It shows what has to be done and in what kind of time frame. A teenager may feel that she is making progress in her life simply because she is moving anywhere at all, seduced by the sheer fact of the movement, not realizing that she may be drifting in circles. Complete the map and she can avoid heading off in the wrong direction simply because she feels that any movement is a good thing.

On pages 164 and 165 are two illustrations. The chart on page 164 contains examples of "The Map to the Big Dream" for two imaginary people, one who is twelve and the other sixteen. In my imagining, the twelve-year-old has a wonderful run and becomes an Internet startup billionaire by the

time he graduates from college. The sixteen-year-old is likewise an overachiever and becomes both a successful execu-
tive and a novelist, and is featured in *Time* magazine. The
chart illustrates the many changes that would take place in
both their lives over the ten years of the road trip, based on
these seven criteria:

Where they live.
How they are educated.
The sports they play.
Whom they love.
Where they work.
How much money they make.
What they accomplish.

Along the bottom of the page you will see that there
are six empty boxes, numbered 1 through 6. In these your
daughter will write down what her life would look like as
she pursues her own big dreams, and accomplishes her various goals and gets herself across the country from Los Angeles to New York. She can imagine how she will change
on the basis of these same seven criteria: where she will live,
whom she will love, how much money she will make, and
so forth. By doing so, she will have a very clear view of what
it will take to achieve the big dreams she has set for herself.
She may find that the trip suits her perfectly, or she may

find that she is not cut out for the Peace Corps after all. Either way, she gets a good look at the next ten years of an ideal life and what she will need to do to achieve it.

On page 165 is a map of the continental United States. The six cities are clearly identified and each has a corresponding box next to it, numbered 1 through 6. These synch up with the six boxes on the chart, and roughly the same information will appear in both sets of boxes. Though this may seem redundant, the chart and the map are just two different ways to look at the same information about your adolescent's or teenager's future, like a pie chart and a graph of the same financial data. (If you need additional copies, or make mistakes, or have nine children, download more maps at growthetreeyougot.com.) Here is how to use the chart and the map:

1. Identify the current year for Los Angeles, two years later Santa Fe, two years later Dallas, two years later Chicago, and two years later Atlanta. Under New York, write the year that will be ten years away. For instance, if you are in 2012, the bottom line of the chart and the map will read: 2012, 2014, 2016, 2018, 2020, and 2022.

2. The easiest box to fill out is Box 1, so start there. Her age, where she lives, the schools she goes to,

what sports she plays, and so forth. Seven facts of her life right now, today.

3. Next, in the New York box, Box 6, your daughter should write down precise details of the life that she would like to be living ten years from now. Maybe she will own her own business, win awards for her work, be quite rich, possibly be married and have a child, work countless hours for her own charity, live in a nice house somewhere, etc. This is the big dream you are fashioning, so try to make it an enormous success in all aspects.

4. In the boxes next to the other cities, begin to identify milestones that will have to be achieved in order for all the details in the New York box to happen. If your daughter wants to own her own successful business, for instance, and live on the profits from it, she needs to get that business started within the next five years, maybe as early as Dallas. Note that achievement in the Dallas city box. If her dream is architecture, and she wants to win awards for her architectural designs by the time the trip is complete, she needs to enter and win small competitions while she's in Santa Fe. Note that detail in the Santa Fe box.

5. Now, as with a cryptic puzzle, gather and fill in the details of your daughter's life, imagining there are seven categories of milestones tagged to each of the cities on the map. Tailor and adjust the various accomplishments that will be required to achieve the big dream your daughter is dreaming of and hopes to live someday.

6. When the map is complete, your daughter will have a view of her life, at least a glimpse of the life that would be required to achieve the big dreams she has set for herself. Now she can get a realistic sense of what everyone, including her, thinks about the plan. Your daughter may decide this is a trip she does not want to take, or may decide she needs to change several details in order to reach her big dream by the time she rolls up in New York.

7. Once there is a final version, I recommend that you preserve the map and put it up on the wall or the fridge or somewhere where it can be seen every day. It will serve to remind your daughter of what may come, as well as how much hard work and good luck it will take to accomplish a successful life and a remarkable career.

The map to the Big Dream

A WAY TO IMAGINE LIFE OVER THE NEXT TEN YEARS

	LOS ANGELES today	SANTA FE 2 years on	DALLAS 4 years on	CHICAGO 6 years on	ATLANTA 8 years on	NEW YORK 10 years from today
ADOLESCENT	AGE 12	AGE 14	AGE 16	AGE 18	AGE 20	AGE 22
LIVES	at home	at home	at home	dorm	dorm	loft apartment
SCHOOLS	7th grade	9th grade	11th grade	freshman/sophomore	junior/senior	graduated
PLAYS	soccer/basketball	basketball	basketball/golf	golf/tennis	golf/guitar	guitar
LOVES	mom & dad	babysitter	girl next door	exchange student	graduate student	mom & dad
WORKS	in the yard	at the neighbor's	Subway	RA	bookstore	president
INCOME	negligible	$50/wk	$150/wk	room & board	$150/wk	Internet startup
ACCOMPLISHES	AYSO champ	spelling bee champ	debate champ	beer pong champ	dating champ	billionaire
TEENAGER	AGE 16	AGE 18	AGE 20	AGE 22	AGE 24	AGE 26
LIVES	at home	dorm	dorm	ugly apartment	nice apartment	first home
SCHOOLS	11th grade	freshman/sophomore	junior/senior	graduate school	lectures	asst professor
PLAYS	basketball/lacrosse	intramural softball	basketball	leg injury	golf	Wii
LOVES	girl next door	lab partner	long distance	local bartender	coworker	fiancé/fiancée
WORKS	Subway	student store	Starbucks	cabdriver	junior executive	vice-president
INCOME	$100/wk	book discounts	$125/wk	$20,000/yr	$40,000/yr	$100,000/yr
ACCOMPLISHES	graduates HS	dean's honor roll	graduates college	writes first novel	publishes it	featured in *Time*
YOUR OFFSPRING	#1	#2	#3	#4	#5	#6
LIVES						
SCHOOLS						
PLAYS						
LOVES						
WORKS						
INCOME						
ACCOMPLISHES						

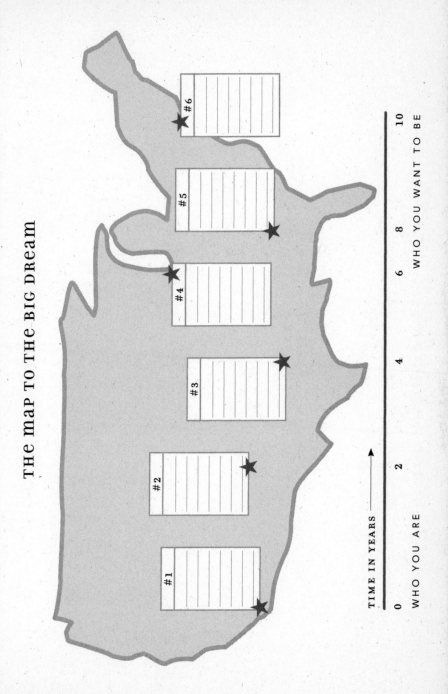

PART FOUR

SIBLINGS COMPLICATE EVERYTHING

It so often happens that just when a child starts to finally feel secure, starts to believe he truly does have a place in your heart, and that everything could be just right with the world, and he can finally start to breathe easy . . .

Then . . . a sibling comes along!? You had another child? You went and threw a big monkey wrench into his careful plans for a perfect life? Really?? What the . . . Boy, oh boy, does that change everything, and change it forever! You think global warming is having a big impact on his world? How about a younger sibling to really throw the balance of energy in the universe out the window?

The persistent grappling that begins on the day you bring the second or third little angel home from the hospital will continue in one form or another for most of your children's childhood, well into adolescence, and will start to abate only in the middle to late teenage years. Having a younger brother or sister brings new meaning to the term "challenging relationship." It is like having someone come over to your house and wrestle with you—for fifteen years.

Sibling rivalry is a polite way to say, "You've got to be kidding me . . ." It's another term for outrage. For no longer being the baby. For being replaced. For having to share everything. For having someone younger and far less interesting around all the time. For having that person always touch your things, things that are not meant to be touched by people that young. For having someone younger read things that are not meant to be read, and never understand fully what the words "Leave me alone" or "Get out of my room!" really mean.

Following are some ideas for keeping the playing field even, the interactions somewhat fair, and the judgments respectful and kind, while considering the feelings of both sides in the heated rivalry that is, and always will be on some level, life with a sibling.

THE THOMAS BELL

When my now ex-wife Antonina was pregnant with our second child, Sam, I took our then six-year-old son, Thomas, aside to let him know that there were going to be some changes ahead. I wanted to let him know that things in his life were going to be a little bit different from now on. I wanted to give him some perspective on his own life as it was coming at him.

I told him that he might have to share some of his toys and that he would not be the only boy in the house anymore, and that soon his world would no longer be his own. He knew that there was a baby brother on the way, but he did not know what this meant in real terms.

One of the most challenging moments in the life of an older child can be the arrival of the younger child. Especially if the parents put the younger child ahead of the older one in terms of time and attention. A simple paradise becomes a complex series of strategies designed to make up for a love that used to be so easy to find. What was me-me-me becomes "When is it going back to the hospital?" Sunday morning with Mom and Dad eerily reenacts the gunfight at the O.K. Corral, with the younger child playing Doc Holliday and the older one playing Wyatt Earp.

What used to be hers alone is now a group thing. Diana Ross has suddenly become the Supremes. They do not call it sibling rivalry for nothing. Who can blame the older child, frankly? She is only trying to make up for the love that was diminished with the arrival of the younger brother or sister, or twins!

If you are having a hard time with this concept, imagine that your spouse comes home one night with a much younger and just as cute version of . . . you! And then your spouse informs you blithely that this person will be staying *forever*. This individual whom you've never met will now share your bed, wear your clothes, eat your food, use your toothbrush, and play with your toys—and by "your toys," I mean your spouse. Before you can even take a deep breath to raise an objection, your spouse quickly adds that you have absolutely nothing to worry about, that nothing will be different, that nothing will change, and of course, that he or she will love you just as much as before. How's that again? How can it possibly be the same? There is another person here! How can you love me just as much? There's more of us and less of you!

Is it any wonder that children have a hard time learning to trust their parents?

I did not want to phony up the challenge for Thomas. I knew that this was going to be a difficult adjustment. But I wanted him to know that I would be there for him, looking out for him every step of the way. I explained that it was one of the privileges of being the older child. I told him that all he had to do was call out for me and he would find me right there next to him. But we needed a sign, flag, symbol, or alarm that he could set off. After a few minutes, we came up with the "Thomas Bell." Obviously this was because his name is Thomas. If your son is Rudolph, it would be the "Rudolph Bell." Virginia would get the "Virginia Bell" and so on. The Thomas Bell was an imaginary alarm that he could ring whenever he felt displaced or threatened by the simple fact of his brother's being on the planet.

I told Thomas that one day in the near future, everyone in the family would be crowded around his younger brother, who would be doing very little to deserve all of the attention, just like they used to all crowd around Thomas when he was a baby and did not deserve all the attention either. I told him that if this day should ever come, he might feel a little left out and overlooked, and that it was very normal to feel that way. But he did not need to feel angry or upset about it. It was very understandable. All he had to do was ring the Thomas Bell and I would be there.

I did not want him to have to taste envy or jealousy at such a young age. Why let those weeds take root in the heart of one so young? I wanted to give him the tool to extirpate it right out of the ground the moment it snarled up at him the first time. That tool was the Thomas Bell.

A year or so later, a big fuss was being made over one-year-old and nearly toothless Sam eating some ricotta cheese—very sloppy and all-over-the-place ricotta cheese. Not doing anything else, just eating the cheese. The cheese was all over his face and the table and his hands and it was pretty cute, and everybody was crowded around him, laughing and having a great time. Then I heard, from across the room, a tiny sound: "Ding." And then silence. Then another "Ding" rang out and I looked around like a seagull atop a deserted pier piling. And there was Thomas, all alone, way on the other side of the living room, looking completely miserable.

From my spot at the table near Sam, I asked him, "Was that the Thomas Bell?" He nodded glumly in reply. I jumped up from the crowd that was busy admiring Thomas's younger brother and practically flew over to him. He was laughing before I even got near him. I kissed his sadness away and asked him what he wanted to do, and we spent the rest of the afternoon locked away with toys and books, throwing balls and telling stories, and he was completely the center of my attention. Just like I promised, without any excuses or reasons why. He did not have to explain himself or examine his feelings, as we both knew exactly what they were.

I did not want that pang of jealousy to have a chance to take hold or otherwise stain his perfect heart, and by providing him a way to recognize it, I do not think it ever did. He had a bell that he could ring if he needed it. He needed it only that one time, and has so far kept most of those sad emotions far from his heart. It never found a way in early, and thus has never found a place at all. He cheers the successes and achievements of his brother and of everyone in his life. Envy has never found refuge in him. Even now, as a teenager, he appreciates the success of others and encourages everyone he meets.

When you are with your children, there are so many sounds to hear. The laughter, the breathing, the happiness, the music of their voices, the clattering of their heels and toys on tiles, the songs they love, the passion they feel, the sounds of life and their lives echoing everywhere. Among the cacophony, just in case, remember to listen for the ringing of the Thomas Bell.

ON THE PRIVILEGE
OF BEING
THE OLDER CHILD

꘎

There have to be distinct, noticeable advantages to being the older child. The older child has earned this right not only because he or she was the first one in line but also because he was your parenting experiment, your very own guinea pig, the one upon whom you tried out your unproven theories and strategies. Then, on some or even many levels, he was displaced by all who followed, and expected on some or even many occasions to be an assistant parent.

The older child must be completely respected by his parents and must be *seen by his siblings* as being completely respected by his parents. When you show him complete respect, his younger siblings will know only to show him that same complete respect. The younger children should regularly witness their older sibling treasured and honored and grow up to hope that they too can earn that same kind of treatment at some point in their little lives. This creates a chain of expectation that will be a trellis for the growth and maturity of the younger children.

The older child's relationship with you will serve as a model to the younger siblings. Sometimes it will be a model to follow, and in other times it will be a model to avoid. Sam is probably a better student than Thomas because he remembers all too vividly watching Thomas get into constant trouble for not studying enough. Sam would never want to be spoken to like that or punished like that. So he studies.

The fourteen-year-old and the eight-year-old should never be held to the same standards. They are two completely different people at two completely different times in their lives. The rules and regulations of the house must be adjusted for the age of the children trying to follow them. In ways that are little but important nonetheless, privilege the older child, for instance with a later bedtime, a right to choose the restaurant, even the right to lock his door on occasion. Your older child deserves as many of these tiny rewards as you can think of. Remember, he was first. He survived. And do not make them dress the same. Ever.

He is also helping you raise the younger children as part of his childhood. He is giving up playtime and time with his friends so that you and the other rug rat can do a quick run to the Home Depot. But he is also learning how to be a parent by helping you with your parenting. He is watching you to see how he is supposed to watch his brother or sister. He is assuming responsibilities beyond his age or ken—and this should be a recognized fact that earns him more something . . . allowance, sleepovers, time playing video games, whatever it is that brings him a little joy. If he works for you as an assistant parent, and does good work, recognize and reward him for doing so.

At the same time, the older child must know that he is never be allowed to use these privileges you have provided as a platform to bully or dominate the younger children, whether by word, deed, implication, suggestion, or seemingly innocent inference. The bullying older brother is my least favorite of the clichés of family. When Thomas was younger and I would catch myself doing something boorish, I would criticize myself by saying it was a "bad older brother" thing to do. I wanted that moniker to be in his consciousness when he caught himself doing something boorish. I wanted him to *want* to be a great older brother. I wanted the skills and qualities of being an older brother—the looking out, the extra kindness, the prescience, the anticipation of a need—to be familiar to him so that they would be readily available for all his dealings with the world, not just with his younger brother Sam. You can get a read on what kind of parent your child will be by watching him or her interact with a younger sibling. Kind is kind.

Thoughtful is thoughtful. Selfish is selfish. If you do not like what you see, make the change now. Alter the course and nature of his relationship with his siblings and his parental destiny by challenging and changing the way he respects and interacts with his younger brothers and sisters.

Every day with your children, you are setting the tone for your family, creating and re-creating the style of your parenting. It will and should change constantly, mutating to allow for the changes that your children are going through and that you the parent are going through every day as well. If you think you haven't changed, take a look at your wedding pictures. Who are those people? Your children grow a little smarter every day, adapting to the new world around them, employing the many new things they learn at school, at sports, at dinner, on television, and of course on the Internet. The interactions between you and your children will be a little different every day, and this is all to the good, they *should* change every day. Differences and discussions between parent and adolescent child should grow less fractious and more gracious as time passes. As your child and you both grow a little bit older, the need for insistent and incessant parenting diminishes, and hopefully your child becomes more of a pal and less of a responsibility. You will find that you can share more and more of your truths with him, about your own adolescence, your time in college or the military, even your days being single, if you want to go there. If it all works out, you may get to be friends at some point too. I mentioned earlier that my mother and I achieved this compromise and new balance in our relationship when I was fifteen. Even now I can remember that glorious day. It was an emancipation. No more little boy— on any level. I was a young man from that point forward. With my brother long gone to the Navy, where he would spend years in the belly of a nuclear submarine, I had become the older child. She recognized that I had earned many new privileges and allowed them to be.

Rate your sibling
(as a sibling) on a
scale of 1 to 10

❧

A few years ago I was stuck in a line at Disneyland—one of those circuitous, irrational mazes that wastes lots of time while you inch along. Right ahead was an adolescent brother-sister act who had been squabbling for at least twenty minutes. Finally, when I could not stand it anymore, I engaged them both and asked where they were from and how they liked the park, California, and so on. Then, when the moment was exactly right, and of course with the approval of the parents standing right next to them, I asked the boy to rate his sister on a scale of 1 to 10, explaining first that 10 would be the most perfect and amazing sibling, while 1 was something quite the opposite.

He looked over at her, smiled, and begrudgingly gave her a 6. She was standing right there and was most surprised by this answer and possibly had her feelings hurt a little too. She might have been eleven and he might have been twelve, just opening their eyes to their dawning adolescence. I then asked her to rate her brother on the same scale and she gave him a 9. He was very pleased with himself and so that immediately brought her up to a 7. I asked him what else it would take for her to get her number up even higher. His answer was immediate, direct, and to the point. "I want her to keep out of my room," he said. There we were, at Disneyland, thousands of miles from their house, yet he knew exactly and precisely what she did that bothered him. He was carrying it around with him like a marble. I turned to her and asked if she would be willing to stay out of his room in exchange for getting her rating up to an 8. She replied, "Sure," in an easygoing manner, as if to say, "If that's all it takes, that's easy." She then said she would move him to a 10 if he was nicer to her friends.

The exchange, it turned out, was a first for both of them in that the assessment of each other was fair and honest and delivered without hurtfulness or unkindness, accusations or insults. The squabbling immediately stopped. The animosity faded from red to pastel. Simply by allowing each one's opinion of the other to enjoy a little sunlight and cool wind, the irritation immediately uninflamed. The conversation was an emotional salve for both of them. My favorite moment of the whole few minutes happened when their mom, who had been listening intently but not interrupting, flashed me a smile and a big thumbs-up when she was sure that her children were not watching.

By teaching adolescents to "rate" what goes on in the

world around them, we give them a tool that does two important things. First, it allows them to better understand and give context and texture to their universe, and second, it shows them how to effect change in that world, and how to make it better for themselves without making it worse for anyone else.

A child's view of his or her sister or brother can change on a moment-by-moment basis, depending upon who took what from whom most recently and other matters of territoriality and self-protection that consume adolescents and teenagers on a regular basis. One way to find out what's really going on is to ask your son to rate his sister (as a sister) on a scale of 1 to 10, then turn to your daughter to rate her brother (as a brother) the same way. One is Siskel, and the other is Ebert, and the film they rate is each other.

Explain that 10, in this case, is the perfect sister who does no wrong and may be headed for beatification and then directly to sainthood after high school. And 1, in this case, is a girl who has much room for improvement and who just might be considered for the lead role if they ever remake the film *The Bad Seed*. This exercise, and the exchange of ideas afterward, will give you and your son and daughter a chance to speak about things that might not be working for them, at least insofar as their sibling is concerned. You must be sure to listen to all of the reasons why they have rated their sibling the way they have and pay complete attention to the details they provide. If your son and daughter have trusted you with their views on each other, give them the best of yours in return by listening without rancor or judgment. *The most important part of the conversation will take place when you ask each of them what it would take for their brother or sister to get his or her number up.*

You will be surprised to find that it is often something quite simple that is causing the greatest annoyance or irritation. He may tell you that she always goes in his room and looks through his things, while she may say that he always embarrasses her in front of her friends. These are easy to fix, and in the fixing you will show your children the art of compromise and détente, and how to work out their differences with some kindness and understanding.

If there is friction between your offspring, and you want to get them involved in solving the problem themselves, start by asking them to rate each other and what it would take for them to give their brother or sister a better rating. The ability to assess and self-assess will provide a long-term value, leading to better relationships throughout their lives, and better tools to resolve the inevitable disputes that arise between siblings in the present day and the years ahead.

seven ways
to keep the peace

֍

In the sibling battles and skirmishes that define your children's daily life, would it not be ideal to have fairness doctrines and guidelines at the ready, just to keep détente in sight? Rules that every child knows by heart, that dictate the tenor of the interaction, that apply equally to every child's relationship with every other child in the house? Here are some possibilities that limit the reasons for territoriality and arguments between your beautiful children.

1. ONE DIVIDES, THE OTHER CHOOSES
   (AKA "YOU SPLIT—I PICK," ETC.)

This is the simplest way to keep everything very fair and balanced, regardless of age, weight, height, heft, brawn, brainpower, or other differences in ability. The child who breaks the cookie in half chooses second. The one who did *not* break the cookie chooses first. The one who distributes the game pieces is not the first to roll the dice and play. This maxim applies across the board in all situations—food, books, any benefits or advantages, time with Mom, time helping Dad in the yard, whatever. It is valid in every situation where something needs to be shared or otherwise divided.

2. 3-2-1

Three choices narrow to two, and then narrow to one. Here's how this works: The family is deciding where they would like to go for a movie or dinner or what rainy-day games to play. The parent or elder presents three possibilities for any activity. This should be the widest possible array or the children will not feel the fairness that this rule is trying to provide. The youngest child narrows the three choices to two by choosing the one he wants plus one other that he wouldn't mind so much. The oldest child then makes the final selection and thus everyone has had a part in the decision.

3. POSSESSION ARROW

To simplify and speed up changes of possession in college basketball, and avoid wasted time with too many jump balls, the NCAA adopted the possession arrow, which alternates from one team to the other, pointing to which team will get the ball the next time there is a disputed change in possession. You can use this rule as a way to balance things between your children, keeping the more aggressive child from making all the decisions and enjoying too many benefits. First "thing" goes to Johnny, next one to JoAnne, then back to Johnny, then back to JoAnne, and so on. If this is not perfectly clear, please watch more college basketball.

4. ANY ARBITRARY CRITERIA

Pick whatever random criteria you would like, as long as it is clearly perceived as fair by all concerned, to determine which of your children will choose or receive the next benefit for that particular day, or make the next key eating decision, or take which ride. Choose anything you like as long as it adds randomness. Try names by alphabetical order, soccer jersey numbers, maybe astrological signs, or rock-paper-scissors. This keeps any one child from getting too much of a good thing at the expense of his or her sibling(s).

5. HALFTIME, BATH TIME

This rule saves many discussions regarding when children should bathe and why, who hardly played at all today and doesn't need a bath, and all of the other excuses that your children want to present to stay out of the tub. Everyone has to bathe at halftime of whatever game or sport or film is on. When you get back home, walk in the house and quietly announce: "Halftime, Bath Time" to note that this rule is in effect. Watch a game or movie or whatever, but take a break at halftime and every child in the house has to bathe before going back to watch the game or movie.

6. CLOSEST TO THE BALL

In any game that family or the children are playing, the person closest to the ball has to retrieve it when a throw or kick goes astray. This saves much agony over whose fault it is that the ball got thrown, kicked, or batted, or otherwise has gone away. The person closest has to go and get the ball. No exceptions unless you feel like being really, really nice.

7. WE CAN STOP ANYTIME YOU LIKE

My boys and I play a lot of sports. I want to keep them well versed so that whenever they decide which is most important, they will have many choices. Not surprisingly, the trunk of my car looks like a display window at a Sports Chalet. Baseballs and baseball gloves, a football, a couple of old tennis racquets, some soccer balls, cones, two full sets of golf clubs, and shoes for all these activities. But no matter what we're playing, when we're done playing that particular sport, we're all done. No chastising, no challenging of their stamina, no grief whatsoever. On to the next activity. We stop anytime they like.

THE SHARE PLATE

Sharing is such a one-way street for the older child in the house, the adolescent or teenager in this particular diorama. It is a falsehood and explains why the word has come to have such negative connotations over the years. "Share with your brother" really means that the older child has to give some of her cool stuff to the younger one. The younger one is a kid who probably has a snot running down his lip, cannot appreciate whatever it is, and will probably give her a sneer when no one is looking, as if to say, "I told you you had to share with me . . ."

I can almost guarantee you that nothing that belongs to an eight-year-old boy is of the slightest interest to a fifteen-year-old girl. Nothing. So there can really be no sharing. Sharing is when both sides give up something they like. She does not want to play with his frog, or watch him try on his Halloween outfits, or "share" another game of Chutes and Ladders or Candy Land. She wants to get back to texting, the Internet, skipping homework assignments, and has no interest in doing anything that would associate her in any way with the boy in the next room. Her idea of sharing with her brother is when he leaves her alone.

So there is the Share Plate. This is the best way that I know to demonstrate to children and adolescents of all ages what sharing is, so that all can see that there are costs and benefits, and that sharing is best when everyone gives up an equal amount of something they like. The Share Plate is a dining exercise, particularly useful when eating in a restaurant. When the food comes, ask for an empty plate. It sits at the middle of the table, and everyone contributes some of their dinner to it. Everyone can try what everyone else has ordered. Simple. Effective. Easy to repeat. Easy to understand.

For the rest of the meal, there is the Share Plate, bearing witness to the concept that yours is a family that shares.

SIBLINGS, GIFTS, and GIFT GIVING

❧

The world has gotten much more complicated, and along with that, so has gift giving gotten that much more complicated. Many houses already have too much stuff in them, too many extra and unnecessary luxuries and doodads. It is difficult to get your adolescent or teenage child a gift that has meaning and significance, provides joy, shows that you love unconditionally, does not cost a fortune, and at the same time does not ostracize or distance the siblings.

The best gifts are those that the siblings wish they could get—and likely may get on their next birthday or holiday. With siblings in the house, give gifts that reward and encourage, that anticipate and appreciate, that empower and ennoble—maybe a gift that only you can give. Here are some possibilities:

- Boss Day. The birthday celebrator gets to make every key decision for the whole day. Not rudely or obnoxiously, mind you, but she does get that power. Where to eat, what movie to see, what to put on the pizza—every available decision is hers. This gives her a taste of the responsibility that comes with making all the big decisions as she gets a good look at how her choices impact the rest of the family. Important discoveries for later on. This is not a better gift than a new iPod or iPad, but it can still be a winner.

• A Perfect Twenty-four Hours. What is it that your adolescent or teenager would most like to do if he could organize his own most perfect day? What would he consider to be the most ideal, the most memorable, the most remarkable day? Build that day, or at least as close to it as you can possibly get, and that is your gift to him. Set a budget, whether huge or infinitesimal; this is not about breaking the bank. The joy is in planning, considering, and dreaming about it. The anticipation of the amazing day itself is half the fun.

• A Complete Pardon. If your adolescent happens to be in a state of punishment on a particularly important birthday, possibly consider letting him start over. Let that be your gift. He gets a clean slate, a 0–0 won/lost record, a suddenly unblemished past. Give him a gift of forgiveness that he will never forget. Return his phone, put the battery back in the Wii, let him start this new year of life with a complete pardon of all outstanding punishments and obligations that grew out of past transgressions.

- One Year's Allowance, in Advance. What adolescent or teenage child doesn't need a little spending money? Look at this gift as an exercise in financial trust. If your son sticks it all in his savings account, that says much about him. If your daughter blows it all on shoes, that says much about her as well. Either way, things will be revealed, and a great gift will have been given. Be sure to take a 20 percent discount on the total amount because you are paying it all up front.

- Somewhere Unusual—Something Brand-new— Just Us. Life being what it is, possibly it has been a minute since you and your adolescent went off somewhere just as a twosome. Not the whole family, just the two of you. Depending on your means and what opportunities are available, this could be an afternoon at the zoo or a weekend golf excursion, a baseball game or a very long afternoon at a favorite museum. The best and most effective use of this rule—as well as what will make it most memorable—is if the destination is completely new to both you and your child.

- Rule #5: Call me, no questions asked. This is one

of the greatest gifts you can give your adolescent or teenage child, and it is explained in greater detail elsewhere in this book (page 248). The foundation of Rule #5 is this: Anytime, anywhere, your children are somewhere they do not want to be, for any reason whatsoever, they can call you and you will come get them, no questions asked. They are forgiven in advance. If they fibbed to get there, or forgot to tell you they were going, it does not matter. There are no consequences! What a gift this is for newly adolescent children on their birthday . . . to suddenly know what it is like to be trusted, and rescued when it is needed most.

FUN AND GAMES
WITH SIBLINGS

꧁

When Thomas and Sam were growing up, we spent a lot of time in the company of their cousins, Elio and Anthony. I often got the boys all to myself, and the times I loved most were when the boys were still boys, kind of, and when we all got to just hang out together, looking for something fun to do. There is an age range of ten years among the four boys, so this added to the challenge of keeping everyone interested, anticipating, looking forward to, and of course enjoying our time together.

Anthony, Elio, Thomas, and Sam were great to hang out with, and these were amazing times for me too because I got to be a boy again. I got to go back in time and do things I never got to do the first time around. Okay, so I was older, I shaved, and I had a driver's license. So what? All that that did was allow me to facilitate our adventures with greater ease, like taking a trip to the movies, or skiing, or golfing, or going wherever we wanted to go. I was just another boy in the group and that was all I really wanted. I did not want to be the disciplinarian, the jailer, or the rule enforcer. I just wanted to be one of them, a part of the group.

But in order to keep everything as fair and balanced and fun as possible, there were very clear guidelines that I created and employed to be sure that everyone—not just me—was having a great time. Here are five ideas I employed most often to keep fun times fun when playing with a mixed bag of siblings, nephews and nieces, and cousins of different ages, or with any group of children where competition was natural, and fair not only needed to *be* really fair but had to be *seen* as being really fair.

1. SQUEAKY WHEELS VS. RUSTY GATES (I.E., FAIR AND BALANCED TEAMS ARE A MUST!)

Because I was so much bigger than everyone else, it was easy to create imbalance in any competitive team event that we were playing. Seeing how easily this could happen, I came up with a concept that rarely failed. I would shout out "Squeaky wheels versus rusty gates!" as another way to say that there was to be no whining, and that teams, whatever they turned out to be, had to be fair and balanced teams. Nothing is more important when playing with children and siblings than playing on balanced teams. Children instinctively spot the imbalance in an arrangement and react immediately: "That's not fair, you got Johnny . . ." or "You guys are already twice as good as we'll ever be . . ." These are the battle cries of the younger child recognizing how impossible the game is about to be or will become or is already. To ensure balanced teams, the adult should always be the teammate of the youngest or least able child or children in the game. This allows the younger children to feel immediate relief and support in their battle against the older children. A side benefit is the team sport ethic that the older children in the game must use in order to beat the adult. Playing on fair and balanced teams as a child will create in all of the children the expectation of fair and balanced teams as they get older, during their adolescence and teenage years, in friendships, school, life, and everything else. The younger children will almost never feel that the odds are stacked against them and they will never feel defeated before the game has even begun. The older child will likewise never feel that he got "stuck" with his younger and possibly less talented brother or sister or cousin. Every game we played, whether it was Madden NFL, the annual Thanksgiving Turkey Bowl, soccer, basketball, or baseball, the balance was always assured by the fairly balanced dictum of "Squeaky Wheels vs. Rusty Gates."

2. CAMP TOM-TOM

Another way of saying "All Fun, All the Time." Sometimes when I was with the boys, we would make an agreement among ourselves that, for the time we were together, there was to be nothing undertaken that was in any way responsible or good for any of us. No trips to the Quilting Museum or learning the words to the Gettysburg Address. In other words, for a few hours at least, there would be no worries at all—about school, punishments, reading, or chores . . . no worries about anything, just hanging out, having a good time together. If it was not fun, we did not have to do it. It was not "You can go to the movies when you finish your chores." It was "Let's go to the movies!" It was not "Do all your homework and then we'll play football." It was just "Who's ready for some footballlllll?" Camp Tom-Tom was a slice of juvenile heaven. Whether for an hour or two or even for a whole day, if we could pull it off, the idea was to set aside time to do nothing but be together and have easy fun. This is clearly not an all-day, everyday kind of activity, but for certain Saturday afternoons or lazy summer evenings, there is nothing better than Camp Tom-Tom.

3. NIGHT WALKS

This is a post-dinner trek through the neighborhood with one adult and lots of children, with no set purpose or mission other than to walk around and get back in one piece. There are simple rules, of course, such as no disappearing and no trespassing, but not much more than this. The beauty of the night walk is that it can easily turn a group of children into a pack of cohorts out exploring the neighborhood and keeping it safe for future generations. My boys still talk about night walks as one of the many high points of their adolescence and very early teenage years.

4. TAP TAP

In my first book, *Parking Lot Rules*, the Tap Tap Rule describes a mechanism that allows a younger child to escape a predicament when playing with older children or adults. All he or she has to do is shout out "Tap Tap!" and the game, activity, teasing, tickling, even the conversation, comes to an immediate stop. No explanations required. Game over. While this is a valuable tool for children of any age, once there is an adolescent or two in the room or on the field—and significantly more skill, weight, and heft in every tackle, wrestle, swing of a pillow, or race—this rule is a lifesaver. Yes, for the child, but just as much for the adult.

Thomas's friend Matt added forty pounds over the summer of his junior year in high school and he nearly broke my hand when we saw each other the next fall at orientation. I screamed "Tap Tap!" as the knuckles on my hands began to merge into one giant ball of cartilage. Tap Tap builds a fail-safe way to stop some interactions from getting out of hand (so to speak) before anyone gets hurt or loses too much face.

Of all the rules, Tap Tap is the one that Sam uses most often. Anytime he wants something to come to a full and complete stop, whatever it is and for whatever reason, he says "Tap Tap" and that's the end of it. A few days ago on the golf course we were having a conversation about girls and boys. He threatened to tell me everything he knew about the subject. I looked over at him and said, "I'm not interested in having this conversation right now. I'm golfing." He persisted, and after a few more sentences I looked over and said, "Tap Tap." It put an end to it, right then and there. He had used that rule so many times himself that he knew exactly what the words meant. Fantastic to watch him stop himself too.

5. THE FOUR FUN-DAMENTALS: LOTS OF POINTS, SHORT GAMES, NEW TEAMS, PLENTY OF RULES

No matter what you are doing that involves lots of individuals, especially if there are adolescents and teenagers in the mix, the responsibility of the head guy or girl is to keep everyone interested and percolating. Nothing keeps adolescents more entertained than games that have lots of scoring, that conclude quickly, and that have a multitude of easily followed rules. Think of the activity as a living video game. Who wants to spend twenty minutes getting everything set up and just so? Get with the points. Get with the clock. Get the rules in order and get started. And no matter what, the teams should change personnel frequently so that no one ever loses too often or by so much that he loses interest in continuing.

Among the more interesting games that involve lots of points and plenty of rules to entertain a roomful of adolescents or teenagers are Knee Football (the game is played with everyone on their knees), Tricycle Time Trials (a Big Wheel tricycle is raced downhill through a punishing slalom course of soccer cones and trash cans), and Wacky Fighter Jets (a swing set is used as a flight simulator for a plane in deep trouble— while everyone lobs in footballs and tennis balls until the pilot bails out). The premise of each game was so much fun that we were playing every one of these even before all the rules were agreed on.

But with new rules showing up at a moment's notice, lots of points being scored, team personnel changing every ten minutes or so, and very clear winners and losers being announced, the time flies by and everyone stays engaged and interested—which is not easy to do with adolescents and teenagers!

PART FIVE

PUNISHMENT VS. UNDERSTANDING

The purpose of punishment is to change behavior. The more change is needed, the more direct and challenging the punishment should be. Punishment is a technique to get your adolescent child to do things differently, but it cannot be the only tool in the box. There must also be compassion and understanding, a willingness to look at both sides of an argument, an ability to consider extenuating circumstances, a ready supply of forgiveness, and a small cache of second chances. Being an adolescent's or teenager's jailer is no fun at all and can hurt an otherwise beautiful friendship.

In *Parking Lot Rules*, there are several essays on this subject. Though originally conceived and written to deal with preadolescent children, it turns out that they work very well with my teenagers too. The best of these are "The Truth Reduces the Punishment by 90%," "The List of Joys and the Threat of Discipline," "Bad News First," "Start the Conversation Over" and "Almost Always Skip the First Thing That Comes to Mind." If you do not have that book, summaries of these essays can be found at www.parkinglotrules.com.

Here are some ideas on how to change a specific behavior of your children without changing everything else about them.

PUNISH WITH KINDNESS: WAIT TWENTY MINUTES

Easy to write, hard to live. Admittedly, this guideline requires remarkable self-control. But at the same time, if you can find that self-control, this rule will encourage and allow a better child to emerge. It will show your adolescent or teenager that she enjoys your complete respect, while at the same time helping her maintain her reserves of self-respect.

Keep in mind that disciplines and punishments have a simple purpose: to change a behavior. So what's the hurry? Why the big rush? Once you know you have to enforce a punishment, you simply wait twenty minutes before deciding what that punishment should be. The heat of the moment will have passed. There will be no rush to judgment. Your decision will not be fraught with emotion. You will have given yourself the opportunity to coolly and logically decide and administer the best punishment to achieve the desired result.

For your child, that twenty minutes will go by like twenty

years. These will be tension-filled and anxious moments. Adrenaline will be swooshing through the bloodstream. Eyes will blink way too many times. Stomach will churn with anxiety. She will know that something is about to go down that probably won't be altogether pleasant. This is all to the good. During these twenty minutes she will have time to think about whatever it is that she did, and just how stupid it was.

Change the behavior, not the person. Give yourself twenty minutes to decide what the best punishment should be. Then inform what it will be, and when it will begin. Coolly. Calmly. Totally under control, i.e., terrifyingly. In so doing you will punish with kindness, the best and most respectful way to do the least joyful of parental tasks. Punish, but wait twenty minutes for your emotions to get out of the way of your decisions.

THE BIGGEST TREE
IN THE FOREST

※

Any arborist worth her bark cutter will tell you that one of the most amazing things about trees is how they form a community. She will tell you how they work and band to-gether, how they communicate, how they meld their roots into a communal system to attain water and nutrition from the soil. She will tell you that this system of the strong help-ing the less strong is key to the survival of the grove.

The ultimate proof of how well their system works is how trees act and interact in emergencies. Yes, they actually have an emergency plan. During times of drought or fire, trees work together as a copse, as a family, as a community, as a village. At times like these, the biggest trees actually reverse the process of taking from the soil, and let their life juices flow down toward the ground and into the roots of the smaller trees all around them that may not be as strong or as developed. In other words, the big trees actually feed and nourish the littler trees. The bigger the tree, the more it provides, and the more is expected of it.

If your daughter has brought a crisis to your house, or is in the middle of a private one all by herself, your first reaction may be to turn away from her, reject her, push her back, and push her down. But now may be the time when she needs you more than she has ever needed you before. A punishment may be the very last thing that this situation calls for, no matter how much it is deserved. You may be angry with her, disappointed in her, upset with the choices she has made that have brought about the present crisis. But you should try to realize that this is only a first reaction, and that she may not be strong enough to survive without you and the love that *only you* can provide her.

Imagine that she is like a little tree, her own reserves running low, her own water supply nearly nonexistent, as the fire that is burning in her life just gets hotter and hotter. She may not know how to ask for more of you, and she may not know that she *can* ask you for more. She may be so embarrassed by her situation that she refuses to discuss it with anyone. Or worse, she may think that everything is fine.

Share even more of yourself in her days of crisis and woe. Help keep her fed and alive and nourished until the problem has passed. Anticipate her weakest points—and balance them with your strengths and strong suits. Let into the soil all around her your patience, wisdom, kindness, love. These are just some of the things that she is looking for from you—whether consciously or unconsciously, knowingly or unknowingly.

Be there for her when you are needed the most, when the danger is hard upon the family, when the fire is raging all around you. Let the best of you seep out and into the family and community that are looking to you for protection and nourishment.

Be the biggest tree in the forest.

DELAY BY TWO WEEKS SOME IMPORTANT EVENT

✦

Let's talk about Thomas's lateness. It is that legendary.

The Knights of the Round Table have fewer stories told about their gallantry than there are tales of Thomas's lateness. His penchant for delaying his exit from any one activity to begin any other activity is the least endearing thing about him, and there is nothing more maddening. For many years—say, from ages nine to sixteen—he simply would not change. He holds several school records for the most tardies. Whatever is the absolute opposite award of being on time every day, he received that in elementary school. Middle school was three years of rushed entrances, mumbled reasons why, allergy attacks, several blows of the nose, and finally the realization that he did not bring his completed homework. High school was not much better. Short of using a cattle prod and pulling him by a ring in his nose, there was nothing that was going to change this habit. He was always late, the way a bill collector is always early.

When his friends were scolded for being late to a soccer practice or a choir rehearsal, they would simply say, "I was waiting for Thomas," and the teacher or coach would shake his head ruefully and say, "Well I can certainly understand that excuse, Austin." School, soccer or basketball practice, movies, dates, whatever it was, he simply could not or would not get there on time. Even getting to airports and getting on planes on time was difficult, and we almost missed flights and ended up doing the "late for my plane" dash through the airport.

I think he was able to be so blissfully unconcerned because everyone else was so terribly concerned. It wasn't really his problem that way.

I could hardly wait for this rude and obnoxious habit to change. Finally a game changer showed up, a reason for him to try to change himself, a once-in-a-lifetime opportunity walked in the door. Finally there was something he cared more about than he didn't care about being on time. Finally there was something that I could use to demonstrate to him the absolute rudeness of being late and the absolute importance of being on time. It was his driver's license. He was fifteen, turning sixteen, and the possibility of getting his license loomed ahead of him like a desert oasis.

And why shouldn't it? A driver's license is the gateway to freedom, the passport to everything and everywhere. It is the proof of one's ascension to the rank of responsible young adult. I was thrilled to be able to point out that responsible young adults are never late. They are always on time. Always.

With the license making such an impact on his life, I came up with a mechanism to show him how important being on time *had* to become in his life. It went like this: From that day forward, every lateness he succumbed to would delay by two weeks his right to a driver's license application. Simple, clean, easy to understand, easy to implement. Five minutes cost two weeks. An hour cost two weeks. A total no-show cost two weeks. Everything that was an appointment counted into the tally. Every time he had to be *anywhere*, not just school, but a doctor's appointment or a dinner date with me, or basketball practice, or an SAT class, it counted. Every lateness delayed by two weeks his ability to submit his driver's license application.

To avoid any doubt, and as a way to underscore the significance and importance of the exercise, we kept a record of the latenesses that were counted against him. The record was a large piece of paper, tacked to a wall, that listed plainly, for all to see, exactly how many times he was late, and at the beginning he was late a lot. True to form, he was unable to get anyplace anywhere near the time he was supposed to be there. But once the tardies began to add up, and his license was months and months further away than it should have been, he started to take the whole punishment business more and more seriously.

Thomas's birthday is in November, and he got to apply

for his license in May, if that gives any indication of how difficult a habit this was to break. Even with that much hanging in the balance, he could not grasp what he was losing until he saw almost everyone else in his junior class driving around town. "Ben Stevens got a license?" he yelped one time, "And with only one good eye . . . ?" It was not until he began to take full responsibility for his lateness that he could begin to control it. When it finally affected his life more than anyone else's, he began to understand. He discovered that the only way to get a driver's license was to change his behavior. The purpose of punishing an adolescent or teenager is to change his behavior, nothing more, nothing less. Thomas, not anyone else, had to make the change in his behavior. Finally he did, thank God.

Delaying the most important milestone in Thomas's young life was the only way to completely and absolutely get his complete and absolute attention. It made him realize the importance of being on time like no other metric could. We were able to change one bad habit without changing his nature or anything else about him that we already loved.

HAD WE THE CHANCE
TO DO IT OVER AGAIN

※

Many families have seen their children get caught up with drugs or alcohol. Often they ended up, as a result, having to take extraordinary measures to retrieve those children from the addictions or other complications that resulted from the behavior, often at great personal suffering and expense. I spoke at length with several who endured this sad circumstance, of course once the family had emerged from the shadows. I asked them all to look back on their lives and kindly identify what they would have done differently if they had had a chance to go back in time and do it all over. These are their answers.

TOM—Chores and Responsibilities Around the House

Tom raised his son in a much more affluent environment than he knew as a child. Maids and gardeners and handymen were always all over the place, leaving nothing for the son to do but watch everyone else do the work. With all of his free time he developed several bad habits, culminating in a marijuana distribution network at his high school, leading quite naturally to a juvenile court appearance, and an addiction to alcohol and marijuana. After several years, while his son was in and out of a few rehab programs and treatments, Tom did a lot of soul-searching and self-examination and came to a simple conclusion: He had made life too easy for his son. There were not enough responsibilities. Tom believes that his fundamental mistake as a parent was not giving his son the chores and regular duties around the house that he was required to do growing up. He wishes that he had given his son more to do on a daily or weekly basis that would have allowed him to know greater self-respect and the pride of contributing to the family's well-being.

MARCUS—Sports Sports Sports/Busy Busy Busy

Marcus got it completely right with his second and third children. The calendar in their kitchen looks like the ESPN2 schedule—every day has several events to be contested, whether baseball, basketball, hockey, or soccer. You name it, his second and third children are doing it, sometimes morning and night.

But he was not so wise with his first son. He let that one "be a boy" and "have some fun" and let him determine his own schedule much of the time. He did not want to be the "pushy" dad. He has since realized that being the pushy dad would have been the better choice. Once adolescence came to town, his first son was not in the habit of being busy and was not all that interested in sports or hobbies or hanging out with his family. Suddenly he had a lot of time on his hands and a lot of nothing to do with it. Since he could not find things to do, things found him. Things like drinking, smoking, all-day video game parties, filling open hours with whatever came along. After several meetings with school principals and several failed drug tests, Marcus found a tough-love high school somewhere in the mountains of Utah. It turned out that his son had a problem that had been previously overlooked and possibly misdiagnosed. He did not know it but his son had ADD and was self-medicating. The world was moving too fast for him and that was his way of slowing it down.

Marcus had three pieces of advice to offer on this subject. First, notice the early signs and respond to them immediately. Do not assume that things will work themselves out. Things rarely just work themselves out. Second, look for the things that are making your adolescent or teenager's life difficult and excise them, or replace them with better habits and more acceptable activities. Third, fill the calendar. Have as many sports and camping trips and museum visits and other activities in your child's world as you possibly can. Teach your children *how* to be busy by *keeping* them busy. Not just doing things that you love, by the way—eventually this would be torture for them. Be flexible in your mutual pursuits. As soon as they discover a new interest or talent, let it become the thing you do.

RALPH—There Are No *Little* Changes

Ralph's daughter seemingly transformed overnight. She switched up on everyone. New friends, new wardrobe, new approach to life. She was a very nice girl, doing well in school, or so everyone thought, and then it was like she fell off a cliff. One day everything about her was different. Boys, clothes, study habits, makeup, friends. The change was complete. Her adolescence was like a license to drop out of her old life and drop into a new one, and she took full advantage of it. But by the time anyone in the house actually noticed, it was too late. She had practically mutated—like a friendly caterpillar into an unhappy moth. What had been a few stray embers from a careless camper had become a forest fire burning a swath of black misery across the hillside of her family's life. Her grades went straight to hell and, with them, so did everything else. By the time her transformation was complete, she had effectively dropped out of high school and stopped speaking to her parents. There were suddenly lots of boys, but fortunately, no pregnancy. Grades went from A's and B's to C's and D's. Makeup went from light and natural to severe and near Goth.

Looking back, Ralph wishes that he had noticed the tiny shifts in her universe before they had coalesced into an overhaul of her life. He wishes that he had seen the drops of water coming through the cracks in the dam before the dam broke. Ralph's counsel was that parents need to stay intimately involved with their adolescent children, especially as they begin the change. Nothing is too small to bring up, no detail is worth overlooking, everything is worthy of at least a stab at conversation. Get down to the level of quarks, leptons, and microbes, if necessary. His advice was to be ready for anything to happen. Ralph learned too late that anything *can* happen.

RONNETTE—Nothing Else We Could Have Done

Ronnette and her husband did everything possible within their world to keep their amazing son on track. Both had stable careers and made good money, both of them left lots of time for the family. She and her husband were married for twenty-plus years, sent their son to great schools, helped him with his homework, and were there and present every single day of his life, up to and including the days when he became an addict and an alcoholic. I asked what she would have done differently, and she surprised me when she said, "Absolutely nothing. We were great parents. The problems he faced were something he just had to go through . . ."

Obviously there is nothing at all to learn from her experience or her explanation, because she did not think she had done anything wrong and would not look at herself critically. But I have included her odd story as a further example that anything can go wrong, at any time, regardless of how right everything seems.

DOUG'S WIFE—Snoop Mommy Mom

Doug and his wife leave absolutely nothing to chance. They have three daughters, so why would they? They check every call on every cell phone. They call all the numbers they are not familiar with and ask the unsuspecting person on the other line how it is that their daughter's phone has this number on it. They scour the daughters' Facebook pages like DEA agents in Arizona on border patrol. Anything they don't like is discussed that night over dinner. They bought some app that lets them read every e-mail their daughters send out, whether that is legal or not. There is nothing happening in the lives of these three girls that the mother is not intimately aware of. Trying to get a secret past her would be like trying to sneak a pork chop past a wolf. It's unlikely. Like a mama bear looking after her cubs, she is suspicious and unrelenting, and boy, is she proud of it.

Here is all the wisdom that I gathered on this subject:

Be Involved. In everything that your adolescent children are doing. There is no such thing as a nosy question when it comes to these matters. Ask all of the questions that come to mind, even the awkward ones to which you might not want to hear the answers. Their wishes are your wishes, their activities are your activities, and so on. Doug's wife adopted the code name Snoop Mommy Mom and acted accordingly to ensure nothing and no one compromised her dreams for her children.

Be Early and Anticipate. Do not hesitate when it comes time to act. There is no such thing as a small change when it comes to adolescents and teenagers. Notice everything and respond *immediately* to what your instinct tells you is not the right thing. Quickly develop the acumen of a headwaiter at a five-star French restaurant: Anticipate the needs and wants and wishes of your daughter as if she were your very best customer and you wanted her coming back.

Be Busy. Idle minutes become idle hours and pretty soon whole days are going by during which the adolescent child may find himself adrift without purpose. If he cannot find something to do, find something for him. Keep him busy and stay with him as he stays busy, whether walking or running or playing sports or reading or cooking or doing some other new activity you have dreamed up just so that he stays busy. This is also a good way to lose those extra ten pounds.

Be Athletic. The more practice time and game time there is in your child's world, the less wasted time there will be. The rituals of sport are compelling and vital to the building of character and confidence, especially team sports. Leagues and uniforms and banners and championships are a great way to achieve a balance, as is a biweekly father-daughter tennis match down at the park. Generally, lots of sweating is a good sign that your adolescent is pursuing and attaining excellent physical goals.

Be Responsible. Hand out chores like an NBA ref hands out fouls. Clean up the yard, take out the trash, wash the car, walk the dog, move the beehive, yakkety-yak, don't talk back. Whatever you can think of that will give your adolescent or teenager a sense of purpose and pride of ownership in the place where she lives, assign it. If the family can afford to, pay an allowance. If not, let your daughter earn credits toward some major purchase later on. Let her learn self-respect and confidence by earning her place in the family's chain of responsibilities.

Be a Snoop. Leave nothing to chance. Follow every clue and know everything you children are doing all day every day. On the phone, on the Internet, Facebook, Twitter, whatever. If you do not like something, say something. Object to what you do not like, and let your children know that you are now and will forever be impossible to deceive.

when home is no longer an option . . .

If you believe your adolescent or teenage children are putting themselves into difficult situations, whether because of bad choices, the wrong friends, or even failures in your own parenting, or if you suspect that drugs and alcohol are contributing factors, do not hesitate. Get involved. Be early. If the situation has gotten beyond your reach, consider one of the following organizations as a possible place to turn for counsel or advice, or in more extreme situations, an alternative besides your home. While I am recommending a few award-winning facilities below, may I please recommend that you make this choice with caution and honesty about the problem you are trying to cure.

Among the best drug and alcohol rehab programs that work are these:

Alcoholics Anonymous (everywhere)
Sober Living by the Sea (Newport Beach, California)
Sunhawk Recovery (Utah)
Wilmington Treatment Center (North Carolina)
Unity Rehab (Florida)

JUST PUT THE DRAWING
ON THE FRIDGE

❧

Seve is a devoted and loving parent. Most of the time. He provides for his family in extraordinary ways and has amassed wealth that could create a generational change in his family's fortune and fortunes. But because he works so long and so hard and pushes himself to the absolute limit every day, he believes that his family and children should work just as hard as he does, as though their efforts in and at life should mirror his own. With this rubric in place, he has very high expectations for his older daughter, Erica. He expects outstanding achievement from her at school, at home, in her ballet class, and in everything she does in her life. He knows deep inside that she can never begin to meet his expectations, but if by chance she does, he knows he can find another challenge for her just ahead. He told me that he gets upset with his beautiful and brilliant daughter now almost every day, and I could see why. It's like she's starring in *The Apprentice* and he gets to be Mr. Trump. Every time she sees him, it's a new challenge, a new chance for defeat, a new chance to be fired.

I was at their home one morning for breakfast and witnessed an exchange that was unfortunate for everyone. Erica had apparently worked very hard on a paper for school—I think it was on the Peloponnesian War or something else way ahead of most sixth-graders. She had waited until the last minute to get everything done, as a lot of people do, and was racing to get to school on time. She was beaming at her father because the paper was, in her mind, perfect. But as a result of the time it took, there was not enough time to get her room cleaned up, at least not to her father's complete satisfaction. He was yelling at her as she left to get on the bus, and she had tears in her eyes as she looked back at him. In point of fact, maybe her room was a mess, but come on, now . . . Why would that minor detail take precedence over the chance to celebrate her intelligence and creativity? Why would a made bed be more important than a completed homework assignment? A small housekeeping rule broken in the name of a great grade at school seemed to be a fair exchange, at least to me. But not to Seve. He piled this accusation on top of some others, including failing to help with the dishes the night before, not helping fold the laundry, and so on. He dug Erica a hole from which she was not going to get out very easily, if at all, and certainly not in the time allowed that rushed morning.

When she got home that afternoon, Erica had found her

balance and was once again very pleased with herself. In addition to getting the paper in on time, she got an A on another project and had extra-credited herself into a B+ in science. What she did not know was that her father had received an e-mail from a teacher in the school who complained that Erica was "bossy" and dominating the other students in a speech class. She could not know that her father was like a trap waiting to spring. She greeted him warmly but he was not warm in return. She noticed instantly that something was wrong and went immediately on the defensive. Her tone changed and so did his, and within a moment, a pitched battle was taking place and raised voices were echoing throughout the house. This lasted the rest of the evening.

Seve was unhappy with himself but did not know what else to do. Meanwhile, his daughter was learning to dislike him a little more every day because he had developed the habit of being repeatedly and overly critical of her. His expectations were so high that she knew she would never meet them. He constantly compared her effort and activities with those of other children, whom he hardly even knew, and this broke her heart even more.

Many afternoons he mixed himself a cocktail of impossible expectations and unreachable comparisons, and drank it down to the last drop. He felt the buzz and jumped all over her, again and again, day after day. Without knowing how or why, he was building a wall between himself and his daughter that would turn out to be much harder to tear down than it was to build up.

He meant well, but so what? Do you think she cared about that as she sat alone in her room, crying softly, wondering what it would take to please this man?

⁂

As parents, we should be careful to guide our adolescent and teenage children, but never defeat them. Lead them to the places we want them to go, but never break their hearts or spirits getting them there. Recognize their great accomplishments but never use their accomplishments against them, and never make them compete with themselves. When they make a mistake, yes, it is okay to detail the negatives, but once it's done, it's done. When they succeed, we should spend time on that fact. We should ask questions and gain for ourselves a detailed understanding of the hows and whys of our children's successes. We should try to be part of their lives' solutions by being a part of their lives' inspirations.

Okay, so Seve's daughter did not clean her room. Why? Because she was achieving another far more important goal that her father set for her—getting the most out of her education. Okay, so his daughter was a dominating speaker during a debate class, but maybe that is because she had more to say than anyone else in the room. But in the meantime, she worked extra hard on an extra-credit project and got her grade up in science. These things have to balance each other out somehow.

Erica showed her father an accomplishment and he dismissed her efforts. It hurt her feelings, for good reason. All she wanted was for him to recognize how hard she had worked on her project. She wanted his respect. She wanted him to realize that she was doing it all for him, just the way he wanted her to. She wanted him to be proud of her, just the way he had been proud so many times before, when she was much younger and life was much simpler. She wanted to see him smiling at her.

She just wanted her dad to put her drawing on the fridge.

no Reason
To ever Hit

❦

Many years ago, before marriages and children, back when my many-year career in the music business was just in its third year, my friend Len invited me to join him at an all-day Man Festival. This was one of those gatherings that you read about where several thousand men gather and bring their own drum and plan on doing a lot of beating on it. The main speaker was poet Robert Bly, who had written a touchstone book about men being men titled *Iron John*.

Although there were probably many memorable things said during the course of the day, I remember only one thing that happened. I did not have children yet, and I was years from meeting the woman who would bear my sons, but that day I made a promise to myself and my family-to-be, whoever they turned out to be, that I would never do to my child what was done to my friend Len by his father in a moment of uncontrolled anger.

At one point, Mr. Bly asked all of us to turn to the guy

next to us and admit something. Something embarrassing or shameful that we had kept hidden or secret for many years. I think the hope was that by sharing a few gory details, we could all rid ourselves of the things that were lessening our manhood. I had nothing to confess, only because I wear my heart on my sleeve anyway and my life is like an open book at a public library. But not so with Len. Apparently he had been keeping lots of secrets.

He told me a sad and extraordinary story about himself. He was a tall, skinny fifteen-year-old boy, on the verge of his manhood, just stepping out into the world as both a storyteller and filmmaker, starting to think about colleges and the life that awaited him. All in all, a great kid. But somewhere along the path, he got into an argument with his father, and he was probably a little rude while standing up for himself and what he wanted to do with himself in the years ahead. His father was offended by something he said or the way he said it and ended the conversation quite suddenly by slapping his son across the face with an open hand.

With tears springing to his eyes, Len described himself. Shocked and disbelieving. Humiliated. Shamed and ashamed. He cried as he told me. I heard the voice of the teenage boy, wrongly accused, and punished by the man who was supposed to love him more than any other man in the world. The injustice alone was enough to make me wonder how someone does that, but the most terrible thing was that the slap was *still* a part of Len's life, was still making him feel terrible. He was still outraged. All those years later and it had never gone away. It continued to reverberate somehow, like a tuning fork emitting a low hum. It was still very real to him that day, and to me as I describe it here.

A rude word spoken, a hot flash of anger. A quick rise of temper, and a hand raised to a loved one. Might as well put up a bronze statue in the park—the memory will last at least that long. Those few awful seconds are permanent in the life of the recipient.

As I might have mentioned, I never actually knew my father. I was oblivious to the possibility that some small act of anger could linger for so long. But hearing Len's story made me entirely sympathetic to the life of the complete strangers who would someday become my children. I began to hope that no matter who they were or who they turned out to be, no matter what kind of sons or daughters they were, that they would never have to talk about me the way Len was talking about his dad.

But more than hope, I made a promise to my someday children that no matter what happened in our lives together, no matter what circumstance or situations we found ourselves in, I would never hit them, or even touch them in anger, for any reason whatsoever. It was a big promise and I was happy to make it. I did not want any of my children sitting in a big room somewhere, someday, banging on a drum.

Of course I have kept that promise. Very easily.

Hitting an adolescent or teenager is one of the most primitive and unthinking acts you can ever visit on their little lives. The saying "Spare the rod and spoil the child" no longer has the slightest validity (if it ever did have any), and it has no application in *this* world. We have evolved from that ethic and from those days. Violence only inspires more violence. Children who get hit turn into people who hit. The mind does not have a delete button and the memory of being struck by the person who is supposed to love you forever will last forever. There is no reason to ever let this kind of thing happen to you and your family.

No reason to hit, ever.

no reason
to ever yell, either

❧

No yelling at adolescent or teenage children, either, please. Never, ever. Never, forever. When you get upset, whisper. It is the only way that your message will get through all the noise that is going on in your adolescent's head anyway. Yelling shows no respect and diminishes a young person's sense of self-respect and self-worth. Yelling is a form of bullying and only proves that you, the parent, have completely lost control of the situation you are in, whatever it is. Yelling scares the children and makes the neighbors reach for a video camera. Yelling scars. Yelling accomplishes absolutely nothing, it only reduces and demeans.

Whisper, whisper, whisper. The angrier you get, the softer you should speak. And if you get *that* angry, you probably should not even be speaking. Not out loud, anyway.

Maybe it sounds like a huge challenge, but I promise you that it is doable. My own sons have certainly upset me at points in their lives, and will surely continue to do so throughout their lives, I am sure, but never so much that I would care to disrupt their sense of self and their own humanity long into the future by yelling at them about something they did or said. Possibly I am given to WCSS-ing more than I should, but the more upset I am, the longer it takes me to respond. The more upset I am, the softer my whisper gets. If I ever yelled, it might lead my sons to believe that I do not love them as completely as I do, and that, frankly, is just not worth the risk.

LIAR, LIAR

I throw my hat in the ring almost anytime anybody needs anything. When California governor Pete Wilson appointed me to mentor an inner-city child as part of a partnership of business leaders volunteering in education, I did not hesitate. But I was unable to pick just one child from the class that I was supposed to choose from; I was sure it would hurt every other child's feelings. I asked instead to mentor all thirty-seven.

Using creativity, songwriting, studio recording, and live performance, I showed high-need, at-risk, gang-influenced public school children that there was a positive way out of their situation. During a six-year span, we wrote and recorded songs together and performed all over Los Angeles, at fifty-two events in front of a total of 45,000 amazed people. It started when they were in seventh grade and lasted until every single student had graduated from high school. Thirty-four of the original thirty-seven choir members have graduated from college, and twenty-two attended graduate or professional school. The story of their many successes is told in an award-winning documentary, *Witness to a Dream*, directed by Reginald Brown.

One of the three who did not make it into college was a boy we will call Julio. He was one of the original members of the choir and he was just twelve years old when we first met. Julio lived near the school. His parents had put both of his older brothers through college, so he seemed destined for graduation, college, and even beyond. But the difficulties of life in an economically challenged inner-city neighborhood were proving too much for him to overcome, especially the gangs and their lurking influence. You never really know how difficult life can be for a child in that circumstance until you walk down his sidewalk, study the cracks in the concrete, listen to the sound of the streets, the sirens and alarms, the urban cacophony that wakes him up at night. Look closely at his worn-out shoes: What do they tell you? What seem like simple choices from a distance may be life-and-death decisions up close for the child involved. That was the case with Julio.

Twice during Julio's adolescence I had to go far beyond the normal parameters of a mentor-and-mentee relationship and get involved trying to save both a child and a childhood. I was needed and I knew I *could* make a difference, so I tried to be his one believer. The first situation occurred when he was in ninth grade. Julio was not a great student, and there was increasing pressure on him to live up to his brothers' already significant academic successes and possibly even go beyond those achievements.

One day, a math teacher's handbook, the one with all of the answers in it, went missing. By coincidence, Julio, who was barely getting a D in math at the time, suddenly got A's on several successive tests. He refused to admit that the teacher's handbook was in his possession, despite all the evidence to the contrary. The school administration was trying to avoid making a difficult situation even more difficult, so before he was suspended for refusing to return the book, I was given the opportunity to speak with him. I met him at school a couple of days later when I was there for a choir rehearsal. I asked him if he had seen the Jim Carrey film *Liar Liar*. This is a very funny picture about an attorney, an unrepentant liar, who is caught in a magic spell and suddenly is unable to tell a lie. Julio and I discussed the film and, by extension, the value of the truth. At this point it was a given that he had the book—although he had not yet admitted to it. He seemed to understand where our dialogue was headed. He then said that, for him, the truth was not always an option. Not an option? How not? He told me that he needed amazing grades so that he could get off the streets and away from the gangs at war around him, and that it was also important for his sanity for him to get out from under the expectations of his parents and other family members regarding his education. He was not going to achieve those lofty goals without good grades, and if a teacher's handbook was what it took to make that happen, then so be it. I could not imagine being just thirteen years old and already under that kind of stress. That's how telling the truth was not really an option.

I told him that I understood his difficulties and challenges, because I had somehow survived mine. But I also told him that I have strict rules about certain things in my life. No loaning money, no alcoholics, and last, no liars. I cannot have any of these in my life. Nothing personal, just not so good for me. If he wanted to stay in the choir and continue to have me in his world, he would have to give back the book, accept all of the consequences, and promise everyone that he would never, ever lie again. He would have to be like Jim Carrey in the movie, i.e., be unable to lie. Very gravely, he shook my hand and said he understood, and walked out of the room. A very long three minutes later, he walked back in and handed me the teacher's handbook. He accepted fully the punishments that he was given, which were not insignificant. He also earned my complete respect and kept his place in the choir. For a while it looked like everything was going to work out.

Cut to Julio's senior year of high school. A few weeks before graduation, a teacher's keys went missing, including those to her house, car, and several storage rooms at the school. Julio was the last person seen in the room with the keys. Even so, he maintained that he had not taken the keys and reminded people that he did not lie anymore, ever. But no one believed him. Julio would not change his story, despite the raised eyebrows and doubts that it created. Evidence was stacked high against him and the administration threatened to refuse him a diploma, but still he would not budge. Just as before, the school asked me whether I wanted to intervene.

Three and a half years had gone by and Julio had not told a lie since the teacher's handbook went missing—a fact of which he was very proud. He had also kept his place in the choir and was one of the few students to sing at every single performance we gave. I sat down with him one day and we got right down to business. I reminded him of his promise to me when he was in ninth grade. He said that he remembered that promise and that he had kept it, and that it had kept him out of trouble many times. I then asked if he had the keys.

"No," he said.

"Are you sure?" I asked.

Pause.

"Yes, I'm sure."

"Were you in the room with the keys?"

"Yes."

"Did you see the keys in the room?"

"Yes."

"Were you there when they went missing?"

"Yes."

"But you did not take them?"

Pause.

"No, I did not take them."

"I'm a logical guy, Julio: How can that be?"

A long pause, followed by a heavy sigh.

"Maybe I wasn't the only person in the room," he said at last. Duh, I thought.

It dawned on me at last that *of course* there had been someone else in the room. The person who took the keys. Julio had made a promise to me and all the choir members and all the teachers that he would never lie ever again, and he was keeping that promise!

"Who else was in the room?"

"I would rather not say."

"Do you know the person who was in the room?"

Another very long pause.

"I would rather not say."

"Why can't you say?"

He just shook his head and said, "The truth is not an option."

Again that same phrase.

"Julio. There is a lot riding on this conversation. There are unhappy people all over this school. There are going to be many sad consequences if you do not say who took the keys."

He said, "There are going to be worse consequences if I *do* say who took them." When I asked him why, he explained his extraordinary dilemma. It was the greatest quandary of his young life, so far. If he said nothing more, the keys would remain missing and he would not graduate. But if he said anything more, he would admit to being a witness to a crime that could put someone in prison for life.

Let's pause for a moment to understand the unintended consequences of a law that meant well but went much too far.

"Three Strikes" was an initiative voted into law in California in 1994 that was designed to put habitual criminals behind bars permanently. It was sold to the public as a solution to recidivism. Three felony convictions would put someone in prison for the rest of his life, no matter what, and judges had no discretion in sentencing. California voters wanted their streets free from the lasting taint of repeat offenders. The biggest problem with the statute was that a marginal lawbreaker could be sent away for life for a trivial crime like stealing a bicycle, failing to show up for a court date, vandalizing a school, or even stealing some keys, just because it was the third strike.

Julio knew that the individual with him in the room who took the keys already had two strikes, and Julio was captive to the belief that stealing the keys to a school and a house and a car would likely be his third strike. That person could possibly go to prison for the rest of his life, and Julio, as the main witness, would be the reason why. Julio believed that if it was found out that he was the first witness for the prosecution, his own life would have little value to the fellow gang members of the boy who took the keys—other than the reward that would be offered for him. Julio said finally, "Graduation won't mean anything if I can't walk down my street and if my family can't live in our house."

What a terrible choice he was facing. Either he tells the truth and he graduates, but without much to live for and probably not a lot of time to live it in, or he tells a lie, breaks his promise, never graduates from high school, and lives a life without much hope or future in it at all. A perfect example of a Hobson's choice. The truth was not an option, and now I really knew why. I got it. Finally. I called the school administrator. When she got on the phone I asked if she would be willing to persuade the school to back down from its threat of no graduation if I could somehow arrange for the keys to be back in that teacher's room within a very reasonable time period. There would be no questions asked about who took what, when, how, why, and so forth. The assistant principal was a very knowledgeable and wise woman, and she also wanted to find a way out of this. So we created the framework for a truce between the parties. If the keys reappeared by four p.m. that day, and not a minute later, the matter would be considered closed and Julio could graduate with the rest of his class, no questions asked. I hung up and asked Julio if he could make that happen. He had about two hours and he said he would try. Just before four p.m., the keys reappeared on top of a desk in the teacher's room.

I discovered many things about Julio that day. I was proud to see that he was unable to lie to me. He had made a promise and kept it. He had found a way to let the truth work for him, not against him. He had told the truth and it had literally set him free. He was able to protect and defend his family and still graduate on time with the rest of his class. It was a great day for him and his family. Unfortunately, it was one of the last great days that he and his family would have together.

Julio did not fulfill his life promises after high school, and ended up getting into a great deal of trouble as a result. He was the only member of the choir who was not accepted at a four-year college. He got involved in drugs and protection, creating his own alcohol, and other vagaries of inner-city gang life. Soon his entire body was covered with tattoos and then, sadly, he went to prison. I continued to communicate with him while he was away and have stayed in touch with him during the years since he was released. I have been trying to help him find employment, but it is a whole different challenge when one has a felony conviction that has to be explained in a job interview.

He told me that if he had kept telling the truth, he probably would not have gotten into all of this trouble. He would not have done the things he did, and he would not have dishonored his family. I looked him in the eye and told him that Liar, Liar could be a way to start all over again, today, if he wanted to, and it would give him another chance at a better life.

He smiled, almost ruefully, and shook his head. I looked past the tattoos and the innocence lost, and got a last glimpse at the adolescent boy he had been when we met.

When dealing with an adolescent, while it may appear that a crisis is small and manageable, try to recognize that it can become quite serious in no time. Try to never diminish the severity of any challenge to the peace in your adolescent's life. If it is a big deal to him, let it be a big deal to you. It's that simple. If it scares him or intimidates him, try to understand why as you help guide him through it. If it rocks his universe, acknowledge its significance and let it rock yours too. Never scoff at or diminish his reaction to a situation. Never be shocked by his naiveté or his inability to deal with it, whatever *it* is. Never laugh at his attempts to fix it. If your son failed some major assignment or missed a key deadline, stand next to him when he seeks the teacher's or coach's forgiveness. When an adolescent child feels a threat to his peace, a challenge to his quality of life, friction on the journey, and panic setting in, let him believe that you can help, because you always have been able to.

As the parent or elder, coach or teacher, you must never underestimate the enormity of the difficult challenges facing your adolescent in just getting through every single day of her life. It does not have to be life-threatening to be life-changing. The larger her crisis looms, the more she needs you. If her crisis overwhelms her, she needs you even more. Try first to be understanding of the reasons why she is panicked, then try to console her, and, last, try to solve the problem. Show respect, always, to your adolescents and teenagers in their difficult situations. Be sure that your efforts to parent, guide, counsel, and mentor are always respectful, kind, loving, forgiving, and, most important, understanding of the difficulties that they face, regardless of how simple those challenges may appear to you.

RULE #5: CALL ME, NO QUESTIONS ASKED (YOU ARE FORGIVEN IN ADVANCE)

When I was in the bloom of my adolescence, arrogant and all-knowing, just fifteen or so, I went to a party to which I should not have gone. This was no place for a kid, especially a naive kid like me. Boys and men older than me, with girls and women older than me, probably doing things people older than me did. I did not need to know about all that just yet. An aura of trouble was hanging over the whole evening like a wet and close fog. Too much alcohol, some drugs floating around, a rumor of a fistfight . . . But the biggest problem was that I did not know how to get out of the situation. I was in a mess. I could not call my mom because I had told her a lie about where I was going. I did not want to have to explain how I got to the party or why I had gone without her permission. The guy I got a ride with disappeared shortly after we parked the car and promptly forgot about me. He was very comfortable with adult women and was probably having the time of his life. Meanwhile I was out of place and scared and alone, just hoping that he would reappear and get me the hell out of there. He did not and I spent hours on my own, trapped in a cage of my own careful design. To use Shakespeare's cloquent words, I was hoist with my own petard. It was an unforgettable night for all the wrong reasons.

When Thomas was turning sixteen, I wanted to be sure that he would never know that feeling. Since I could never forget it, I wanted to be sure that he would never have to experience it. So I invented a mechanism that would get him out of any situation that he did not want to be in. It is Rule #5: Call Me, No Questions Asked. No matter where he is, no matter how or why he got himself there, no matter anything at all, if he is ever somewhere he does not want to be, all he has to do is call me and I will come get him. *There will be no questions asked.* Anytime, anywhere. *It does not matter.* He is forgiven in advance.

I will not care why he went, how he arrived, where he found out about the event, what the hell he was thinking, or who told him it was going to be a great party. I will not care about the people he is with, or if he was drinking, or about any of those details. No explanations will be necessary; that can all be discussed at a more opportune time. All that matters is that he gets out of wherever he is and whatever he is doing, and gets himself home safe and sound. No punishments or lectures. Nothing else matters, and nothing else is important. Safety and being safe at home come before any explanations.

It has been my experience that adolescents and teenagers will foolishly back themselves into strange and unlikely corners. They will tell a little fib in order to cover a slight indiscretion. They will then need to fabricate a little flimflam to keep that small indiscretion from getting out into the world. Next thing they know, a whole lot of truth is being denied, and a web of mistruth gets very tangled very quickly simply because someone neglected to just come clean early on. Yes, the best bet is always the truth, but that is not always clear to adolescents and teenagers. Sometimes they find themselves in terrible situations because of it as well.

But if hiding the truth is what prevents an adolescent or teenager from calling his parents to come and get him out of a party, or some other unfortunate situation, then the truth has gotten in the way of its whole purpose. The truth, in a situation like that, may just have to back itself up and accept that it has become of secondary importance *at that moment*. The truth is not that important if it is endangering the safety or welfare of your treasure, your son or daughter. Even if he told a lie, it would be much better to have that adolescent or teenager safe at home. The chance of real harm befalling him, out there alone in the world, simply because he is afraid to tell you the truth, is just not worth the risk. If fear of punishment is a motivation that keeps your daughter from calling you when she needs you the most, you may need to examine your emergency procedures.

Thomas has used this rule twice. There was much anxiety on his part when he called me the first time to say, "Dad? Remember that rule? Number 5, I think . . . ?" I was asleep but immediately woke up and asked where he was. I wrote down the address and jumped in the car. I had been waiting months for this chance. I felt like Batman trying on a new Batsuit. Ten minutes later I pulled up in front of someone's house. Parents were of course nowhere to be seen and there were kids and alcohol and fighting. Shrubbery had been uprooted and there might have been a car on the lawn. It was mayhem. Thomas was standing apart from all this, his eye on the passing cars, looking for mine. When he finally saw me, and saw that it was true, that there I was, that I had come to get him just as I promised, he actually burst out laughing. He jumped in the car and said, "Dad, I'm so glad to see you. . . ." We went for waffles.

Give your teenagers the gift that keeps on giving. Prove to them that you trust them, and trust in them, and that you will understand if they make a little mistake now and again but that you would rather they be safe and unafraid before anything else is even considered.

Rule #5. Provides forgiveness in advance. Gets your child home safely.

coda

You would think that, after all these ideas have been laid out before you, there cannot be much more that needs to be said on the subject of raising amazing teenagers. Well, there is not *much* more, but just these few thoughts that I could not find a home for elsewhere. They did not quite fit well within the confines of these chapters, yet they each guide my parenting or mentoring in their own unique way.

These are three disparate items, which serve vastly different purposes. The first essay is based on what my father once said to my mother, something she never forgot, and made sure to tell us many times. It became her policy and philosophy in raising us. The second essay addresses the central issue of college and how to prepare to go, or not go, depending on your child and what he or she may be ready for at this moment. Last is a questionnaire, which may help you better understand what is going on with your formerly innocent little angel, and why your child is acting like that all of a sudden, and how you can stay close while he or she is trying so hard to stay so far away.

you cannot keep them

By the time your little darling is shaving her legs with regularity or your little man is shaving his chin just as often, there is not a heck of a lot left for you to do. Your job is very nearly finished. You are like a shipbuilder whose only task remaining on the to-do list is to smash a bottle of champagne on the hull and launch. Your chance to influence with wise counsel or practical advice is pretty much over. The past is about to be the past, and that includes childhood and all those thousands of experiences you shared. You will have (hopefully) given all you had to give. You will (hopefully) have lost your mind only a couple of times during the course of these last several years, and quickly apologized and asked for forgiveness and put some emotional salve on it right away. Either way, the first quarter of your child's life will be over very soon.

So it's almost time. You cannot keep them. They fly away and begin their own lives, attend to their own dreams, their own careers, their own families, and, someday very soon, their own children. Their connection to you will always be there, but it is about to change, significantly and forever. You can do little about it but hope that they will never forget the love, sacrifice, kindness, wisdom, patience, hope, nurturing, and time you so generously provided.

I sincerely wish that your adventures as the parents of adolescents and teenagers will be uplifting and memorable, uncompromising and life-changing. Enjoy the ride, it goes by so very fast.

TO COLLEGE OR NOT TO COLLEGE

Thomas is turning nineteen in a couple of days, and adolescence is a distant memory. His teenage years are about to come to a conclusion, like a great book I enjoyed reading and wish could go on just a few more chapters. There is still a mist of body spray in his bathroom occasionally, but he has left all that behind him—intellectually and emotionally and in every other way too.

Maybe I am still caught up in the reminiscence of all that we had and all that we were. But it seems like only a few months ago I sat in a big overstuffed chair with eight-year-old Thomas in my lap. We were watching Notre Dame play football and I was trying to plant in his head the possibility that he could go to that wonderful school someday, or any other of the magical places on my list, all amazing institutions of higher learning. I thought I was pointing out something very easy to see, like a beautiful sunset or a flock of pelicans.

As we watched coach Lou Holtz foam at the mouth and running backs jook and jog and career for touchdowns, I said, "If you go there, you can watch *every* game in person." To cement the image in his head, we saw *Rudy* at least fifteen times. It never occurred to me that he would *not* go to Notre Dame or might not even go to college at all. Perhaps I missed some of the early signs . . .

Thomas was among the tardiest students in the storied History of Lateness in his middle school and high school. He slept through his SATs. Twice. Thomas applied to four-year colleges only after I hired someone to fill out the applications for him. Talk about not interested—his self-descriptive essays in the applications were brief sentences such as "My dad wants me to go." Not surprisingly, he was rejected by everyone.

And he couldn't have cared less. But finally, after a lot of sweat and tears, and frankly, a lot of begging by me, he got into a college. I did not know it at the time, but the only requirement to get in was a credit card. Santa Monica College feeds students to both the University of Southern California and the University of California, Los Angeles, at a record clip, but only students who are willing to do the hard work and beat out the rest of the students who are trying to make the same transition. Thomas took one class, found the teacher to be pompous, and did not understand why I so badly wanted him to go. He truly disliked it, and asked for a year to think about it, to get on his feet and figure things out, ". . . like the European kids do, Dad." Finally, I said okay.

As the year was half through, and it was time to start applying to colleges all over again, we had a heart-to-heart that was unforgettable in its time and place in both our lives.

Thomas and I were sitting down for dinner at a restaurant near the house, and I was starting to build up to my usual all-too-familiar harangue about him gathering his strength, bearing down, putting his nose to the grindstone, applying to good schools, getting back on track, and so forth, on and on.

But as I looked over at my son, my mind drifted to an article I had read the day before in *The New York Times* about a girl from Los Angeles who attended one of those prestigious Ivy League schools, who was not going to be coming back home. She apparently had not been ready for college, but had not known it. It was way too soon for her to leave home, but she was caught up in the dream. She was planning to continue her education at some point, and all her friends were going, and it had probably seemed like such a good idea—at the time, anyway. She got through nine weeks of college and that was it. Rather than disappoint her parents, she chose another option, and took her own life. The article described the scene of all in attendance at her funeral, standing breathless in the rain, not knowing what to say or do other than cry for the girl, for her parents, for the life unlived, the heart unloved, the gifts not given, the risks not taken, the lifetime not enjoyed, the world that would never know her.

Thomas knew none of this, of course; it was all just like a flash of lightning in my head. But when I focused back on him and what he was saying, he was telling me about college and how unhappy it was making him to try to live up to my expectations, how little interest he had in attending, how it just did not inspire him in any way. He was telling me that he was not sure if he would ever want to go. He was telling me his truth. He was speaking from his heart. He looked at me finally and said, "Dad, you have to grow the tree you got." He quoted me, *to me*.

At that moment, all the thoughts and pictures in my head about a lost teenage girl and her family standing in the rain collided with all the love I felt for this young man sitting before me. In that instant I gave up the fight over his going to college. That was it. Game over.

In that instant I asked myself: Why was I pushing him so hard to do something he clearly did not want to do? Why pressure him to achieve something he had no interest in achieving? Why have every conversation end with the same inevitable stalemate as all the previous ones? What was I doing this for? Why was I so busy tearing down the bridges between us?

I gave up my dream of his attending college, and have not looked back.

For Thomas, it was the right decision, for right now. What it will mean years from now, who knows. Thomas is happy. Thomas has a purpose and a point to his life. He has a goal he wakes up to every morning that he tries to conquer all day. All day every day, all night every night. He eats, sleeps, and dreams his passions, and then he sleeps again. He is a good and caring older brother, he is a respected and respectful son. He is now working as a songwriter and producer, a second sound engineer, a track writer, and sometime tea-boy, like the ones you see leaving the Starbucks with cardboard trays full of hot drinks. He makes enough money to get by, well past subsisting. He is in the midst of an opportunity to learn and hone a skill that cannot be taught in any school. You cannot learn to write a hit song; either you have the gift or you do not.

He does what he's told to do and he loves what he does. He gets to work on time, most of the time, and most evenings he stays late, still there crafting something else to please a fickle populace. Every day there is a smile on his face. The old Irish saying goes, "If you can make your hobby your living, you'll never work a day in your life." Certainly, for now, for Thomas, that is true. His hobby is his music.

His creativity is the love of his life. His life is alive and well. I could not be happier for him.

Was this the dream as I planned it? Not exactly. Was this the future as I imagined it? Not really. Do I have doubts about his decision? Several, actually. But my goal is to help him figure out who he is supposed to become, and then help him become the very best version of himself that he can possibly be.

It's not complicated. Just growing the tree I got.

THE QUESTIONNAIRE

The questionnaire that follows is based on one that I have used for the last several years to help write hundreds of letters of recommendation for hundreds of deserving students trying to get into great schools. The questionnaire gives students and mentees the opportunity to provide details about the hows and whys of the life each of them was leading, and has given me a glimpse of their creativity and ability to write and describe what was going on in their lives. The answers have provided insights without prying, and at least some understanding of the challenges facing each individual, so that I could write about each of them with honesty, whether they were applying for a school, a scholarship, financial aid, or a graduate program.

Show this to the adolescents or teenagers in your life. Ask them to fill it out as honestly and completely as they can. There are no wrong answers, just details about how they think and feel and what they care about. It may give you a picture of what is really going on down the hall. Parents should make every effort to avoid judging the child or the evidence that is revealed. If your child thinks that the questionnaire is a trick or an invasion of his privacy, it is unlikely he will answer it honestly.

If you are ever asked to write a letter and help someone else's child move along the path of her life, here are several questions you might want answered in order for you to write something nice about the little minx without telling a pack of lies.

Name: _____

First, middle (or nickname), last

Name of school: _____

Name of favorite teacher: _____

Name of least favorite teacher: _____

GPA: _____ SAT score: _____

Favorite subject: _____

Varsity sports: _____, _____, _____

Clubs: _____, _____, _____

Name your career choice, today: _____

GROW THE TREE YOU GOT

Special awards or honors within the last three years: _____

_____

_____

Special interests or hobbies: _____

_____

_____

Charity/volunteer work: _____

_____

_____

What is the last selfless act you performed? _____

_____

_____

What is the last compliment you received? _____

_____

_____

THE QUESTIONNAIRE

What is your big dream? _____

_____

_____

What is the difference between love and kindness? _____

_____

_____

What is more important, forgiveness or understanding? _____

_____

_____

What makes you unique? _____

_____

_____

Describe the greatest challenge you have faced, and how you rose to meet that challenge:

_____

_____

_____

What is the last book you read that you would recommend, and why?

_____

_____

_____

You have one vote for the greatest song ever written. What is it, and why?

_____

_____

_____

Is there a phrase or philosophy that you have adopted and live by?

_____

_____

_____

Is there anything about yourself you wish you could change?

_____

_____

_____

What is the meaning of friendship? _____

_____

_____

If you could talk for an hour with anyone
in the world, who would it be, and why? _____

_____

_____

Who is your hero, and why? _____

_____

_____

What is your greatest achievement? _____

_____

_____

If you were granted two wishes, what would they be?

1. _____

_____

2. _____

_____

What is the greatest crisis facing our planet? _____

_____

_____

Who was our greatest president, and why do you think so?

_____

_____

_____

alphabetical index of ideas

acknowledgments
and thank-yous

I gratefully acknowledge the following individuals who have helped me with this work, with no order given for importance or significance . . .

Thank you to Linda Newmark, for reading an early version of this book and suggesting its title.

Thank you to Michael Rexford, for reading two early versions of this work, copyediting, prodding, and suggesting many interesting ideas and angles to tell these stories.

Thank you to Susan Raihofer, for reading three early versions of this book and pushing back on every one of them.

Thank you to Joel Fotinos and Sara Carder at Tarcher/ Penguin, for believing in the possibility that good parenting might make all the difference.

Thank you to those individuals at Tarcher/Penguin who have been such remarkable teammates, copy editors, cover art creators, and all-around enablers.

Thank you to Jeff Strader, the arborist who told me many of

the secrets of trees, allowing the essays "The Biggest Tree in the Forest" and "Rocks in the Roots" to come to life.

Thank you to Jeff Gelb, supplier of wisdom and understanding of the writing and editing process.

Thank you to Sam Armato, for your incisive criticism and very high standards of what makes good writing.

Thank you to Steven Moeller, for the good news / bad news reaction to the nearly final manuscript.

Thank you to Thomas Sturges, for reading about yourself and reacting to honestly to what I got right, and wrong.

Thank you to all my believers: Stephanie Liu, Lindsey Lanier, Michael Rosen, Regina Boutté, Arnold Kaufman, Judy Rosenberg, Lizzy Moore, Deirdre O'Hara, Paul Blake, Hugh Martin, Steve Schnur, David Renzer, Zach Horowitz.

Thank you to Antonina Armato, friend, ally, partner, pal, and amazing mother to Thomas and Sam.

Thank you to my pals Robert Ambrose, Tom Beaver, Mark Lipps, Neil and Deborah Sevy, Nancy Armato, Mike Schiff, Tim James, Sheryl Rooker, Marietta Kin, Mike Perryman, Big Dave Landau, Margot Ferris, Michael Erlinger, the entire Richter family, Elio and Anthony Armato, Lee Auerbach, James McMillan, and Kris Munoz.

Thank you to my brother, Preston, occasionally known as PG Sturges, for steadfast support and devotion to my efforts as a writer.

And last, thank you to my dearest Karen. Your recognition and embracing of my creativity have allowed me to explore worlds and dreams I never thought possible.

If you enjoyed this book, visit

www.tarcherbooks.com

and sign up for Tarcher's e-newsletter to receive
special offers, giveaway promotions, and
information on hot upcoming releases.

TARCHER
PENGUIN

Great Lives Begin with Great Ideas

New at **www.tarcherbooks.com**
and **www.penguin.com/tarchertalks**:

Tarcher Talks, an online video series featuring
interviews with bestselling authors on everything from creativity and prosperity to 2012
and Freemasonry.

If you would like to place a bulk order
of this book, call 1-800-847-5515.